LIVING SMART, SPENDING LESS WORKBOOK

LIVING SMART, SPENDING LESS WORKBOOK

Wise Choices that Stretch Your Income

Stephen and Amanda Sorenson

Disclaimer

This book is designed to be a general guide; its purpose is to entertain and educate. The tips and guidelines in this book are supported by research and/or the authors' experience. Not every tip or guideline will apply to everyone. Readers should use good judgment and common sense when deciding which tips they choose to implement.

This book is sold with the understanding that the publisher and authors are not engaged in rendering legal, accounting, or any other professional service. If legal advice or other expert assistance is required, the services of a competent professional person in the field into which the information falls should be sought. Compliance with local codes and legal requirements is the user's responsibility.

Although much effort has been expended to ensure that the information herein is as accurate and complete as possible, this book is sold with the understanding that the authors and publisher assume no responsibility for errors, inconsistencies, or inaccuracies in this book.

ACKNOWLEDGEMENTS

It would be impossible for us to thank all the people who have shared money-saving tips with us and assisted us in various projects in and around our home and vehicles. So we'll mention only a few.

Thanks, Susan and Ed Edwards, for your loving, prayerful support through the years through thick and thin.

Mel and Jane Sorenson and Roy and Elizabeth Springer—you have given us a lasting heritage . . . and so much more.

Bob and Susan Stewart—your willingness to lend a helping hand anytime to "learning country people" continues to mean a lot.

Eastern and Petra Tin—thanks for being kindred spirits with us during life's journey. We value your friendship.

And a warm *thank you* to others who have encouraged us to share what we've learned about living smart and spending less with others.

TABLE OF CONTENTS

1
Build a Solid Foundation for Smart Living

Times have changed. Once an individual could work forty years for the same company and receive a gold watch at a retirement dinner and a nice pension. Today corporations lay off long-time employees and hire younger replacements whose salaries are lower. Salaries are frozen or cut. Families are saddled with debt. Extended families often don't live in the same town or city anymore, so the family support network is less effective. And the huge, growing deficit of the United States government threatens many aspects of life as we've known it. Many people feel helpless and frustrated as they watch their hard-earned money slip away. They work hard to make ends meet, trying to be responsible with what they have and yet can't seem to stretch their dollars far enough.

There's no doubt that we all face challenging financial pressures and that an increasing number of cracks in our financial flooring appear to swallow up our earnings. Yet the situation is not hopeless. In fact, our greatest personal and financial problems are rarely due to outside economic influences. Most occur because we give too little thought to the future as we form our spending habits.

Few of us have had the opportunity to learn about saving money from good role models or through easy-to-understand classes. No one has shown us how to link up financial preparedness and opportunity. Yet we can take control of our finances rather than allowing ourselves to become victims of our finances. All of us can learn to make wiser choices in how we use the money we earn.

UNDERSTANDING WHY WE MAKE THE FINANCIAL DECISIONS WE DO

Whether we like it or not, our upbringing plays a key role in how each of us views money. Some of us received smart financial advice from a parent or relative from the time we first received an allowance or went to the store to buy our first bicycle. We learned what advertisers try to get us to do and how to evaluate various financial options. Or, perhaps no one close to us used money wisely or shared wise financial teaching. Perhaps we lived in a family that was always in debt or one in which there was never enough money to go around. Maybe we learned to work hard to save money but became discouraged because illness or job loss wiped out what we had worked so hard to accumulate.

Why is it that some people can save money and make it go far? Why are other people unable or unwilling to save money and use it wisely? More than individual personality is involved. We each make decisions based on a complex grid of underlying beliefs, habits, and attitudes. These may have developed when we were very young or when we were adults. We may have picked up correct, partially correct, or incorrect teaching on our own. Or we may have learned about finances from a parent, friend, grandparent, business associate, or the books we read and studied.

Because understanding your financial background is helpful as you begin to evaluate your financial decisions, take a few minutes to work through the following financial background check. See what you discover about yourself. If you are married, ask your spouse to complete this on his/her own and then compare your answers. Be as honest as you can.

Financial Background Check (check all that apply)

In my family, money was:

____ spent quickly   ____ always in short supply

____ a source of conflict   ____ spent impulsively

____ spent only after careful thought

____ something we never seemed to run out of

____ other _____

My parent(s) viewed money as:

____ a ticket to happiness   ____ a barometer of self-worth

____ a hedge against disaster   ____ a resource to be used wisely

____ something you can never have enough of

____ something that could always be taken away

____ other _____

When my family needed to buy a higher-priced item, such as a car or an appliance, my parent(s): _____

_____

_____

Explain how this was similar to or different from the way your family purchased lower-priced items: _____

_____

_____

My parent(s) was/were:
_____ well-informed about financial choices.
_____ knew very little about financial choices.
_____ allowed others to make financial choices for them.
_____ other: _____

As I was growing up, I learned that consumer debt is:

_____

_____

When I needed money as I was growing up, it:
_____ was readily given to me.
_____ had to be earned.
_____ was given to me for a specific purpose.
_____ was seldom or never given to me.

Other kids I knew had:
_____ more money than I did.
_____ less money than I did.
_____ about the same amount of money as I did.

Describe how you felt about the money you and/or your family had in comparison to those around you. _____

_____

_____

I opened my first savings account when I was _____ years old.

The money in that account came from:

_____ financial gifts I received.

_____ my allowance.

_____ earnings from work I did for others.

I used the money in my savings account for: _____

_____

_____

My parent(s):

_____ regularly talked about money with me in ways I understood.

_____ seldom talked about money with me.

_____ never talked about money with me.

I wish my parent(s) had taught me that: _____

_____

_____

The person who taught me the most about money was: _____

Looking back on it, he/she taught me: _____

_____

_____

What I learned about money while growing up affects me in the following ways today:

1. _____

2. _____

3. _____

4. _____

If I could unlearn anything I have learned related to finances, it would be:

_____

_____

_____

WHAT PUTS THE SQUEEZE ON YOUR FINANCES?

There are many reasons why individuals and families today have a hard time stretching their dollars. Some of these reasons are the result of choices; others are the result of circumstances. To better understand your situation, darken the circle of each factor that you believe has limited your financial options:

- ○ Loss of job
- ○ Sickness—high medical bills
- ○ Lack of wise financial counsel
- ○ Bad investment decisions
- ○ Consumer debt that isn't paid off
- ○ Educational debt
- ○ Impulse spending on items I could live without
- ○ Unwillingness to wait for the "good life"—wanting things *now*
- ○ Bad business decisions
- ○ High monthly expenses
- ○ Not earning enough money at my job(s)
- ○ Supporting more than one family, such as parents or children from a previous marriage
- ○ Inability to save money
- ○ Unforeseen expenses, including: _____
- ○ Other factor(s):
    1. _____
    2. _____
    3. _____

Are you willing to be painfully honest? Are the factors you have indicated above primarily a result of your choices or of circumstances? Explain your answer:

_____
_____
_____

What do you consider to be your greatest financial strengths?_____
_____
_____

Your greatest financial weaknesses? _____
_____

_____

_____

We *Do* Have Spending Choices

All of us can learn to make wiser financial choices in how we use the money we earn. Each of us has financial options, however limited they may be at present. If you have any doubt about this, consider how much a working person earns between ages twenty-five and sixty-five (forty years):

Monthly Income	Annual Income	Gross Amount Earned in Forty Years
$1,200	$14,400	$576,000
$2,500	$30,000	$1,200,000

Now compute your expected earnings between now and retirement by multiplying your present annual income by the number of years you have until retirement:

Monthly Income	Annual Income	Gross Earnings before Retirement
$	$	$

Chances are, even at your present salary you earn enough money to have some financial choices! If you are in the early years of your career, your annual income may increase significantly, giving you even greater choices in the future.

Do you agree with the statement, "The way we spend our money is a choice, whether we make that choice consciously or unconsciously"? Why or why not? (Be specific.) _____

_____

_____

_____

In what ways have you benefited from past financial choices? _____

_____

_____

Which past financial choices do you regret? _____

_____

_____

What financial choices would you like to make in the future? (Saving for college?

Gathering emergency funds? Replacing a car? Increasing charitable contributions?)

_____

_____

_____

As you use this workbook, we invite you to consider the choices that are available to you. Some of the choices presented may seem so simple that you wonder why we included them. Others may be new to you and require careful evaluation. Some points may even challenge you in ways you don't like.

By all means, remember that this is a no-guilt workbook. Everyone approaches saving and spending differently. We offer no "right" or "wrong" formulas. We merely suggest new possibilities to consider as you progress on your journey of smart living.

2
Make Sound Financial Decisions and Money-Saving Choices

Advertisers spend billions of dollars every year to convince you to buy or lease items you don't need so that you will achieve a certain quality of life, prestige, or other benefit. But as an intelligent consumer, you can take practical steps to control where your money is spent no matter how effective the advertising techniques may be. Remember, you are the only person who can choose to take your own path or a path someone else wants you to take. The proper path will lead you to the right financial decisions and will free you to make money-saving choices.

MAKING YOUR OWN DECISIONS ABOUT HOW TO SPEND YOUR MONEY

Consider the advertising you see, hear, and read. How carefully do you filter it before responding to it? _____
_____
_____

How important do you believe it is to "evaluate every purchase, no matter how small?" Explain your answer. _____
_____
_____

List four reasons why you spend money the way you do. Be honest here.

1. _____

2. _____

3. _____

4. _____

Now determine which of these reasons represent your desires and goals and which represent the influence of others. _____

_____

_____

What positive steps can you take to regain control of where you spend your money, particularly in relationship to the influences listed above? _____

_____

_____

If you were able to save more money and spend what you earn more wisely, what difference would that make in your life? In the lives of others around you? Be specific!

_____

_____

Take Steps in the Right Direction

Our financial choices either lead us closer to or farther away from our dreams. Whatever is going to happen to you in relation to your dream(s) will happen gradually, as a result of the choices you make.

Do you really believe that your financial choices matter? Why or why not?

_____

_____

Remember the future financial choices you would like to have that you listed at the end of chapter 1? Review that list now and ask yourself which ones are dreams of what you want your financial situation to become and which ones are simply daydreams— fantasies that you will never work to bring about. Rewrite the true dreams here:

_____

_____

In recent years, what steps have you taken toward making each of your financial dreams a reality? _____

_____

_____

What steps have you taken that have pushed you farther away from making your financial dreams a reality? _____

_____

_____

_____

Realize That How Much You Spend Is More Important Than How Much You Earn

It's easy to fall into the trap of thinking that our financial condition will improve dramatically if we just get that next promotion and raise—or if we just make a few thousand dollars more each year. The reality is, however, that living smart and spending less has little to do with how much money we make. Instead, it has everything to do with how we spend what we make. Everyday financial decisions either move us closer to our dreams or farther away from them.

To visualize the difference that spending habits can make, consider the following illustration. Susan and Janice each earn $25,300 a year. Susan enjoys spending her money. Janice enjoys spending hers, too, but works to save what she can without being miserly. Notice the differences in how they live and spend the money they earn.

Activity	Janice	Susan
EATING OUT	Eats out once in a while.	Eats out several times a week.
SHOPPING	Compares prices. Will shop in thrift stores. Watches for sales.	Buys at trendy shops. Will not enter a thrift store. Buys on impulse.
CAR	Drives a reliable, older car paid for with cash.	Drives a late-model car leased through a dealership.
FOOD	Generally eats nutritious foods; cooks; seldom eats "convenience" foods.	Eats "convenience" foods on the run; cooks seldom.
HOUSING	Lives in a basic apartment that she shares with a roommate.	Lives in an expensive apartment in just the "right" neighborhood.
BILLS	Pays them in full monthly.	Has growing consumer debt, particularly on credit cards.
EXERCISE	Jogs and swims at the city pool and recreation area.	Has an expensive health club membership.
SAVINGS	Uses a basic spending plan; saves $100 or more monthly.	Spends until her money runs out and says she can't save.
READING	Frequents the library.	Subscribes to eight magazines.

On the basis of this daily spending profile, who do you think will have more financial choices and freedom in the years to come? _____

Do your spending patterns more closely resemble those of Janice or Susan? Why?
_____

Which financial choices might be available to you in one, three, or five years if you continue on your present spending path? _____
_____
_____

Are those the choices you want to have? _____

If not, how might you change your spending habits so that you can benefit from more of what you earn? _____
_____
_____

Who can help you evaluate your spending habits and hold you accountable if improvement is needed? _____
_____

Give Yourself a Raise

Even though we may realize that wise spending has more impact on our long-term financial condition than on how much we earn, it's still nice to get a raise. There are a number of ways to try to increase our income. We can play the lottery. We can convince others to give us raises. Or we can give ourselves a "raise" by figuring out how to spend less money and doing it.

When have you felt that you must earn more money and worked too hard to achieve recognition in the workplace? _____
_____

What were the personal, professional, relational, and/or financial results of your efforts? _____
_____

If you were to "give yourself a raise" by spending less money, how would you do it? List at least two specific things you could do:

1. _____

2. _____

Describe what you think the ideal way to "get a raise" would be:

_____

_____

FACE AND REDUCE CONSUMER DEBT

A fundamental principle of saving money and earning the ability to make financial choices is to not allow your earnings to be siphoned off by personal debt. Consumer debt is one of the most insidious, destructive forces facing individuals and families today. An alarmingly easy trap to fall into, consumer debt promises people a way to fulfill their dreams today—but at a tremendous price. The dark side of consumer debt is that it:

- ○ Erodes and/or destroys financial choices.
- ○ Robs people of self-esteem.
- ○ Feeds a never-ending hunger for more "things."
- ○ Deprives people of the joy of sharing with others in need.
- ○ Reduces future freedom.
- ○ Weakens the ability to ride out tough economic times.
- ○ Places stress on relationships.
- ○ Siphons off money that could be used to reach financial goals.
- ○ Requires that even more money be earned in order to maintain the same level of spending.
- ○ Creates the illusion that people are better off than they are.
- ○ Creates financially induced tensions and fears.
- ○ Can cause the loss of nearly everything people own.

Check off the results of consumer debt that you have personally experienced. Ask yourself whether or not consumer debt is worth the price.

Perhaps you have little or no consumer debt. That's great! But if you are like most people, you have outstanding balances or pay interest on credit cards and other forms of consumer debt. Financial experts say that many people do not realize how deeply in debt they are. The following Consumer Debt Test is the first step in evaluating your debt situation. Again, this is for your own reference—and that of your spouse, if you are married.

The Consumer Debt Test

Credit Cards
List every credit card on which you owe money and how much you owe.

Credit card(s):	Balance owed:
	$
	$
	$
	$
	$
Total Owed:	$

Credit card(s):	Balance owed:
	$
	$
	$
	$
	$

Monthly Payments
List items you've purchased for which you make monthly payments (car, furniture, and so on).

Item(s):	Balance owed:
	$
	$
	$
	$
	$
Total Owed:	$

Item(s):	Balance owed:
	$
	$
	$
	$
	$

Other Outstanding Loans and/or Outstanding Debts

List any other loans and/or outstanding debts. These may include: unpaid bills to doctors, hospitals, dentists, lawyers, or other professionals; school debt; life insurance; amount you have borrowed on your line of credit at the bank; loans from family members or friends; and money owed to the telephone and/or utility company.

Item(s):	Balance owed:
	$
	$
	$
	$
	$
Total Owed:	$

Item(s):	Balance owed:
	$
	$
	$
	$
	$

Now add all of these totals. $_____

Are you surprised by how much you owe? You're not alone. In chapter 12, you will be able to outline a spending plan that can be used to help you get out of debt. For now, we simply want to help you become aware of how much you owe, because consumer debt limits your financial choices more than any other factor. The following checklist will help you evaluate whether or not you have a serious debt problem. Be honest with yourself as you consider which of the following apply to your situation.

- ❑ Before this, I have never laid out all my bills to see how much I owe to whom.
- ❑ Creditors are calling and/or writing me.
- ❑ I buy merchandise I don't want or need.
- ❑ I get cash from one credit card to pay off another.
- ❑ I consistently pay late-payment charges.
- ❑ I might take out a consolidation loan to cover my debts.
- ❑ I can't pay more than the minimum balances every month.
- ❑ I use credit cards because I don't have enough cash.
- ❑ It would take more than a year to pay off all my consumer debts.
- ❑ I keep using new credit cards because the other ones are "filled up."
- ❑ I buy now on credit based on what I haven't yet earned.
- ❑ The total amount of monthly debt I owe is more than 29 percent of my monthly after-tax income, minus my rent or mortgage payment.
- ❑ My financial fears are growing.
- ❑ If an emergency comes up, I won't have money to cover it.
- ❑ I have needed to borrow money to meet minimal credit obligations.
- ❑ Without my "side" jobs, I would not have enough money to keep going.
- ❑ I keep asking for higher credit limits on my credit cards.
- ❑ I have bounced checks.
- ❑ I have given up trying to pay everything off.
- ❑ I really don't like to think about this.

How many checkmarks did you place on this list of warning signs? Although marking a few of them might not be a reason for undue concern, take a hard look at your debt situation. If you think you might be in trouble, take steps now to gain control of your debt.

Debt-Control Action Steps

The following steps will help you regain your financial choices by getting out of debt.

(Other suggestions are included in the book *Living Smart, Spending Less.*) Check off each step as you complete it.

- ❑ Don't spend money you don't have. Cut up your credit cards and start paying cash.
- ❑ Using the spending plan worksheets in chapter 12, set up a realistic spending plan so you can begin to reduce your spending and your debt. Or, renew your commitment to live within the spending plan you already have.
- ❑ Determine which bills are costing you the most money in interest charges and/or late penalties, and which must be paid soon. Then take steps to pay off the bills that cost you the most, as long as you won't incur penalties from other creditors.
- ❑ Continue to keep up to date on your financial obligations, even if it means paying "the minimums."
- ❑ If you can't meet your minimum financial obligations, take immediate action!
  - * Meet with your creditors as soon as you realize you can't pay them. Approach them first. Show them your spending plan. Perhaps they will allow you to make lower payments for a while.
  - * If creditors are already calling you, contact the Federal Trade Commission for a copy of *Fair Debt Collection* and learn your rights under the Fair Debt Collection Practices Act.[1]
  - * If things have gone too far and you don't know how to straighten them out, contact the nearest nonprofit, consumer credit counseling service that can help you develop a financial plan to get out of debt or arrange repayment schedules with creditors.
- ❑ Be willing to sell assets in order to pay off your debts. Check with a professional, such as an accountant or attorney, before you do this.
- ❑ Consider bankruptcy to be your last resort.

ENJOY THE BENEFITS OF SMART LIVING

In *Living Smart, Spending Less*, we list a number of benefits of saving money. These include: trying new things, doing things with family members, sharing with others who are less fortunate, experimenting with lifestyle changes, and living out your spiritual values in a deeper way.

Which benefits of smart living do you most enjoy? _____

_____

_____

_____

Do you agree that when you begin to save money "your challenge will be to use that money in wise ways that reflect your spiritual values"? Why or why not? _____

_____

_____

In what ways have you succeeded or failed in spending money in ways that reflect your spiritual values? _____

_____

_____

_____

Who do you know who has chosen to make financial choices that reflect his/her values and goals? _____

_____

_____

Set up a meeting with that person to talk about financial choices. List three questions you want to ask that person: _____

_____

_____

_____

Remember, saving money isn't a solitary adventure. It often requires interaction with others. Community is important. When we stand together, caring for one another and helping one another get ahead, exciting things happen!

THE FUNDAMENTAL CHOICE

Remember the story about the turtle that won the race against the quick but lazy hare? That's what this workbook is about—turtle power. When you take small but significant financial steps in the right direction, your choices will save you money so that you win the race ahead of you. Let's look at some of the life-changing choices you can make to set your feet firmly on the path toward smart living.

Perhaps the most fundamental choice you can make in living smart and spending less is to live on less than you earn. If you consistently spend as much or more than you earn, you cannot save money and will eventually eliminate most, if not all, financial options.

On a scale of one to ten, with ten being the best, how would you rate your ability to live on less than you earn? _____

Do you consider yourself to be financially disciplined? Explain your answer.

_____

_____

_____

Obviously you can't live on less than you earn without financial discipline. And for many, such discipline doesn't come easily. Which of the following financial steps are you willing to take today if financial discipline is new or difficult for you?

- ❏ Ask a friend or family member to help me understand my finances and hold me accountable to a spending plan.
- ❏ Consider specific areas (large and small) in which I can begin to spend less and better use what I save.
- ❏ View money as a resource that I can manage even more wisely.
- ❏ Admit that I have a debt problem and meet with a financial counselor, wise family member, or friend who can help me regain financial control.

Ten Money-Saving Principles

Once you have chosen to live on less than you earn, you can spend less by following certain money-saving principles. Here are ten principles that can save you money.

Principle #1: Pay Yourself Regularly

A portion of what you earn is yours to keep, regardless of how little you earn. You may be able to put the money you save into long-term investments, or you may need to direct it into debt reduction before you tackle long-term goals.

List several advantages of saving money regularly that are important to you. (You may want to consider the advantages in emergency situations, in riding out tough economic times, in meeting long-term goals, and in reducing debt.) _____

_____

_____

_____

_____

How much money do you set aside regularly (each week or month)? _____
What is the maximum or ideal amount you want to set aside? _____

It's important to remember that even little purchases or expenses—such as paying for use of the automatic teller machine—can rob you of your ability to pay yourself regularly just as easily as larger expenses. When you practice money-saving habits on a regular basis, you are making choices that will make a vast difference in your life and in the lives of others. Identify some optional, small and large expenses that may be lowering the amount of money you set aside regularly. (We've included examples to get you started.)

"Little" Expenses:	Cost/Item	Times/Week	$ Amount/Year
Snacks at work	$.85	5	$221
One fast food combo meal	$3.99-4.99	2	$415-519

Now consider two "larger," optional expenses you could cut. That could save you twenty, fifty, or even hundreds of dollars each month. These could include a health club membership you never use, a payment on a new van (instead of keeping the old van another year), or recreational spending. List them above.

Note: If your situation is particularly difficult at the present time—you've been laid off, for example, and have little money saved—we realize that you'll need to meet your basic needs before you can think about paying yourself regularly. But you can still set small financial goals and work toward them. In time you will be able to make choices that yield even greater dividends.

Principle #2: Don't Mix Up Your Needs and Wants

Understanding the difference between needs and wants is another key to saving money. Although marketing people want you and me to believe that what we *want* is what we *need*, these words are not the same. You can enhance your quality of life in many ways without necessarily fulfilling all your wants. (Let other consumers expand the economy by consuming more and more goods and services.)

Needs vary, depending on people's unique situations. For example, we need a four-wheel-drive vehicle to negotiate our country driveway during the winter; another family may not even need a car. But needs have a way of creating other needs, causing a multiplication effect. Our vehicle needs trips to the repair shop, tires, insurance coverage, and so on.

Wants can become needs out of habit, too. If a television dies, for example, is replacing it a need or a want? Is redecorating a need or a want?

How would you describe the difference between a want and a need?

_____

_____

_____

Illustrate the difference between needs and wants with an example from your life:

_____

_____

Many people today are fearful of financial ruin because they confused wants and needs and ended up with beautiful homes, huge mortgages, and nearly unbearable credit-card debts. Ironically, many people wish they were making choices that satisfy their own needs and wants instead of pursuing the wants and needs others have persuaded them to seek.

As you review your financial choices, describe a time when you confused wants and needs: _____

_____

What have been the consequences of that decision? _____

_____

Do you have to make a decision soon about a want that has become a need? If so, describe your choice: _____

_____

_____

Remember that in distinguishing needs from wants, sometimes it's difficult to separate the two. For instance, is a larger home or a bigger bank account a want or need? The answer may depend on your particular situation. Keep in mind that over time you may be able to save for that larger, more comfortable home or to expand your savings account. With patience and consistent pursuit of the right financial choices, it is possible to make even the financial dreams of your heart happen.

Principle #3: Realize That Making Choices Isn't Always Comfortable

If you are committed to saving money in a balanced way (doing what you can without going overboard and becoming angry, weird, or miserly), you'll stand out in the crowd. You won't stand out as if you are wearing purple hair in a mall. Rather, people will notice something about you, your lifestyle, and the way you think.

When others pull into the parking lot, your car may be a little older than theirs. When they visit your home, they may see it furnished with bookshelves you built yourself. Your utility bill may be half what they pay each month, or less, and you may be better dressed than they are—for pennies on the dollar. If this is your situation, be prepared for flack. Nonconformists always have an uphill battle because people like the feeling of security they have when other people are like them.

So when people want you to do certain things that require more money than you'd prefer to spend, pay attention to what they say to convince you. Usually they reveal their philosophy of spending, with which you may choose to agree or disagree. Worse, they may have a philosophy altogether different from the one they mention and seek to take advantage of you.

Describe a time when another person tempted or pressured you to spend money in the same way he or she spent money: _____

_____

_____

How did you respond? _____

_____

_____

Who—at work, in your neighborhood, in your family—strongly disagrees with the way you spend money? How does he or she communicate the disagreement?

_____

_____

_____

Jesus challenged people's values. Pompous religious leaders of His day looked down on normal "sinful" folks. But Jesus invited Himself to the homes of those folks for meals.[2] When rich people made a show of giving money to charity, Jesus praised the widow who gave two small coins—all she had.[3]

How willing are you to challenge unbiblical values in your life and make changes in your own lifestyle? _____

_____

_____

As you begin to live smart and spend less, how might your values change? (Be specific.) _____

Which habits might you have to unlearn? _____

_____

_____

What new decisions might you have to make? _____

_____

_____

Principle #4: Use Your Skills and Talents to Save Money

Some people are great at fixing things. Others are skilled at sewing, bookkeeping, marketing, or teaching. If you're like most people, you are good at some things and not so good at others. Just because you don't have the aptitude to save money one way doesn't mean you can't save money in another. Thousands of ways to save money await you.

Take a few minutes to think about your skills and the needs on which you spend money. On the upper part of the chart below, list areas in which you are skilled and describe how you could apply those skills to save money. (You might also want to note how much money you could save by applying those skills.)

Skills I have:	How I might use those skills to save money:
Skills I could learn:	**How those skills would help me save money:**

On the lower part of the chart, list areas in which you could become skilled enough to save money if you took classes and/or worked alongside someone who could teach you.

The key to developing new skills lies in believing that you (and your family or friends) can do it and in your willingness to learn what you don't know. Read owner's manuals. Ask for advice. Take courses at a junior college or technical school. And when you're not sure whether you can do something, try it anyway—as long as there is no risk of permanent damage or injury. You may be pleasantly surprised by the results. You'll learn skills that will help you save money, that may become hobbies, or that may provide additional income.

Principle #5: Look for Alternative Solutions

Stores make it possible for us to meet our needs with easy solutions. "You need it; we have it!" they say. But a key to saving money is to think through your problems thoroughly enough to come up with less expensive alternatives that may work even better than store-bought ones. Believe it or not, when you become skilled at not spending money, it's often easier to come up with your own creative solutions than it is to spend money on other people's solutions! Your resourcefulness, sense of accomplishment, and learning will often make a store-bought solution the least desirable choice. Solutions range from finishing partially assembled furniture to a do-it-yourself chore you may be able to complete with the help of friends or family members.

Consider your wants and needs. How might you apply your abilities and resources to develop alternative solutions? (We have included a few suggestions.)

Want or Need:	Ready-Made Solution	Alternative Solution	Savings
Costumes for kids' imaginative play	Pre-packaged costume	An assortment of belts, jewelry, ribbons, and fabric remnants that can be used for a multitude of self-made costumes	$19-49 for one costume vs. $10-25 for an array of remnants, etc.
Bookshelves	Ready-made shelves or a ready-to-assemble vinyl-finished kit	Make your own with new lumber, create an original from salvaged materials, or refinish a secondhand unit	Anywhere from $20 to several hundred dollars

For future reference, what resources do you have that will help you develop alternative solutions? _____

_____

_____

Principle #6: Evaluate What You Throw Away

Look creatively at items you intend to throw away. Could they have another use? Perhaps you have some leftover pieces of wood that are just right for building bird houses. Perhaps you could cut the bottom off that plastic bottle you were about to throw away and use it as a funnel for adding fluids to your car.

List alternative uses for several items that you would otherwise throw away.

Throw-away items: Alternative use(s):

_____   _____

_____   _____

_____   _____

Which persons, families, and/or organizations could benefit from items in good shape that you can't easily put to good use? Use the trash can or landfill as a last resort.

_____

_____

_____

Principle #7: Preserve What You Have Through Regular Maintenance

Routine maintenance is seldom fun. It may mean getting greasy or calling knowledgeable friends and asking questions about subjects you don't fully understand. It may mean buying a tool that's required to do the job correctly. But if you don't do necessary maintenance—or arrange for someone to do it for you—you are likely to end up fixing items under financial or time pressure. This will cost you more money in repairs and/or in purchasing new items to replace the ones that weren't maintained properly.

Take the time now to think about what you own and any maintenance you have postponed or overlooked. On a sheet of paper, list items that need to be maintained and when the maintenance should be done. Then take steps to do what needs to be done.

Principle #8: Ask the Right People for Help

There is an army of people available for you to consult about virtually anything you need to learn. Most people enjoy talking about what they know best—themselves and what they've learned. We have asked people about generators, engines, painting, trees, grass, clothes, tools, greenhouses, plumbing, and so on. And we're constantly surprised by the number of gifted people who freely offer wise advice. By asking for advice, you can avoid making costly errors and give people you ask the opportunity to share the benefits of their creativity and expertise.

Which projects have you been putting off because you don't know enough about them? _____

_____

_____

Write down the names of knowledgeable people who could provide you with the information and advice you need to get each of those projects underway (store manager, friend, family member, manufacturing representative, and so on). _____

_____

Principle #9: Share and Trade with Buddies

Material goods seem to expand to fit the space available—which leads to crowded closets, garages, and storerooms. But there's a plus side to this law of accumulation: other people may be able to lend or give you what you need so you don't have to rent or buy it, and vice versa.

Several rules apply to sharing. First, realize that things sometimes break during normal use, so don't get mad if somebody has a problem with something you lend. Second, communicate ahead of time your expectations regarding the care of what you are lending. (If you want your fertilizer spreader to be washed out as soon as it's used so it won't corrode, mention that.) Finally, consider buying items that you use regularly or use hard, and borrow and lend specialty items or those you don't often use.

Which items might you be able to lend to others? _____

_____

Which items that you occasionally use might you be able to borrow rather than buy or rent? _____

_____

Principle #10: Start Saving Today!

There's no denying that living smart and spending less requires effort. It's easy to put off tasks that require effort, especially considering the pressures we all face today. Yet money seldom comes to us on its own. If we want to build up our financial resources, we must use existing resources wisely, *today*. Procrastination is the enemy of saving money.

Consider this scenario. If you save fifty dollars each month for thirty years and receive a return of 12 percent, you will have $154,050 in thirty years. But if you delay one year, saving fifty dollars a month for only twenty-nine years and receiving the same 12 percent return, you'll only have $136,950. That delay of one year cost you

$17,100—or $46.85 per day. That's nearly as much per day as you planned to invest each month!

Would you ever have guessed that even a little procrastination would be so costly? No matter what the interest rate may be right now, it's important that you start your adventure of living smart and spending less—today!

Have you ever met with a financial planner to map out your financial future? Why or why not? _____

_____

List the specific financial goals you would like to meet (saving for a major purchase, paying off a mortgage, eliminating consumer debt, helping a child through college, building up retirement funds, and so on). _____

_____

_____

_____

What steps can you take today to begin planning your financial future? _____

_____

_____

_____

1. For the booklet *Fair Debt Collection*, write the Office of Consumer/Business Education, Bureau of Consumer Protection, Washington, DC 20580.
2. Luke 19:11–17
3. Mark 12:41–44

3
Shop Smart

Every time you enter a store, open a direct-mail catalog, turn on the television, listen to the radio, see a billboard, or read a magazine, you are confronting firsthand the strategies of business marketers, whose job is to get you to part with your money. They experiment with voices, colors, product locations, signage, package designs, "personalities," and many other elements in a constant effort to discover what will motive you to spend money on their products—again and again.

The bottom line? Whenever you shop, marketing pressures can influence you to spend your money on things you don't need. So it is important that you learn to shop smart and buy according to your needs, your research, your choices, and your spending plan.

PROTECT YOURSELF AGAINST IMPULSE SPENDING

Impulse spending is a common but dangerous habit. To buy on impulse is to buy an item without carefully evaluating the need to buy it, without comparing prices of the same or comparable items, without demanding quality, and without seeking long-term value from the item when it's appropriate.

What is the number one reason you buy on impulse? _____

_____

_____

What do you usually buy on impulse? _____

_____

_____

What do you estimate those impulse purchases have cost you during the past month? Past year? _____

_____

How might you have put those dollars to better use? _____

_____

_____

Do you think your impulse spending is or is becoming an out-of-control habit? Explain your answer. _____

_____

_____

What steps do you think you could take to regain control of your spending?

_____

_____

If you shop impulsively at times, list at least five temptations you need to avoid in order to improve your shopping habits. _____

_____

_____

_____

If you want to spend less, learn to resist spending temptations. Think about the ways you shop and check off the spending habits that describe you. (Be honest!)

- ☐ I am not afraid to say no to a salesperson.
- ☐ I don't allow high-pressure tactics to wear down my resistance.
- ☐ I can't say no to a bargain.
- ☐ I go into a store armed with a list and buy only what is on it.
- ☐ I spend money so I can feel good about myself.
- ☐ I am aware of how much money I can spend on individual items.
- ☐ Before I make a major purchase—a car, stereo, major appliance, furniture, and so on—I carefully evaluate the options.

❏ I've purchased a number of items I don't really need.

❏ I am not afraid to ask my friends/family members for advice about higher-priced purchases.

❏ I understand the difference between my *needs* and my *wants.*

❏ I don't think much about my future financial needs. I tend to spend much or all of my "extra" money quickly.

DO YOUR HOMEWORK BEFORE YOU BUY

Today, as we were writing this, Amanda overheard a woman shopping for a computer. The woman said, "Do you have a no-money-down purchase plan? . . . How many months can I go without having to pay? . . . And I want a 486 computer with four megabytes of RAM and a big hard drive. And I'd like to get it today."

In effect, this woman was saying, "I don't care much about the quality of the computer, its warranty and service, or about how much the whole package will cost me. And I certainly don't want to shop for the best deal. What I care about is not having to pay right away for what I want now but don't have enough money to buy."

Of course, there are better ways to shop. There are even proven ways to save money when you shop. One of these proven money savers is to comparison shop. Whenever you shop for anything other than a low-cost item, it is wise to comparison shop. And the higher the price of the item, the more important it is to compare.

That's part of preparing before you buy. Do your homework first, and begin by comparison shopping. Look at various products, and talk with people who have purchased specific brands. Check prices and determine quality. When you go to a store, don't allow anyone to pressure you. You'll save money and learn much in the process.

List three "higher-cost" products that you plan to buy within the next six months or year:

1. _____

2. _____

3. _____

For each item, run through the following checklists (covering seven categories) to determine ways in which you can "shop smarter." Keep in mind the value of the time you spend comparison shopping in relationship to the benefits you'll receive. Obviously items that cost hundreds or thousands of dollars that you plan to use for five, ten, or twenty years are worth the time and energy spent in comparison shopping. But a small dollar savings may not be worth more than a few telephone calls or visits to several nearby stores.

✓ **Consider Needs Versus Wants.** It's easy to confuse needs with wants, but in order to live smarter and spend less we must understand the differences between needs and wants and make appropriate decisions. These questions can help you evaluate your need for larger (as well as smaller) purchases.

❏ Why do I need this? _____

_____

❏ What are my real reasons for wanting to buy this? _____

_____

❏ What will happen if I do not buy this? _____

_____

❏ How might I meet this need in a less-expensive way? _____

_____

❏ Do other knowledgeable people agree that I need this? _____

❏ If I am replacing a broken or worn-out item, have I considered repairing rather than replacing the item? _____

❏ How much will it cost to repair the item? _____

❏ How successful might the repair be? _____

✓ **Consider Features Carefully.** Do you really need the top-of-the-line model? Perhaps the more basic (often less-expensive) model will work as well as, or even better than, the top-of-the-line model. Salespeople often want to sell you the "latest and the greatest." But when you know what features *you* need, you have the upper hand.

❏ Which features are really important to me? (For an automobile, these might include size, capacity, gas mileage, power of the engine, color, and safety.)

_____

❏ Will a similar product that doesn't have as many features work just as well for me? Why or why not? _____

❏ If not having those features will require extra time and effort, or create discomfort on my part, do the savings outweigh the inconvenience? Why or why not? _____

_____

☐ Which knowledgeable person or product resource might help me evaluate features? _____

✓ **Consider Quality.** Cheaper isn't always better. Remember the time you bought that thingamajig for twelve dollars, smiled all the way home, and then a week later it broke? Stores today are full of poorly made and poorly designed products. As a result, consumers should be wary. When you can, buy quality and take care of what you buy. Don't buy a doodad that will break down each year when a slightly more expensive one could provide years of hassle-free service.

Of course, there are exceptions. Quality often is less important than price if you plan to use something only a few times. But always weigh quality, price, and value carefully. All merchandise is not created equal.

The following questions will help you evaluate your need for quality.

☐ Is quality important for the use I intend to give this product? Why or why not?

_____

_____

☐ How long do I plan to keep the product? _____

☐ How often do I plan to use the product? _____

☐ What will I gain from a higher-quality product? _____

_____

☐ Which publications might have compared this product to other similar products?

_____

☐ What do their findings reveal about the quality of the product under considerattion?

_____

_____

_____

☐ Which experts could I call to discuss the product's overall quality and repair requirements (repair shops, service managers, professional users)? _____

_____

_____

❒ What is the repair history of this product (if it has been out a while) or its manufacturer? ❒ Excellent ❒ Good ❒ Fair ❒ Poor

❒ What servicing or maintenance will this product require (replacement parts, cleaning, etc.)? _____

_____

_____

Is the product designed to be user serviced? If not, where must the servicing be done? _____

_____

✓ **Consider Price.** If pricing is important—and it should be if you want to spend less—keep in mind that you can cut price two ways. One is to negotiate. The second is to be patient and wait for sales (discussed in the next section). First, let's consider how you can lower the price by negotiating. Just because the product has a price tag on it doesn't mean the dealer won't reduce the price (particularly at the end of the month). Obviously many items, such as those in a grocery store, are seldom open to negotiation. Larger-ticket items, however, often are negotiable, although that fact may not be publicized.

Remember, selling is a game of sorts. Sellers have goods and services they hope you or someone else will be willing to buy. But if people don't rush to buy a product, what happens? It sits in a showroom or warehouse and costs the seller money—an increasing amount of money the longer it remains in inventory.

Negotiating is part of an overall strategy to reduce the price.

Evaluate which of the following may help you to purchase your larger-ticket items for less:

❒ How much can I really afford to spend on this product? _____

❒ If I plan to make this purchase on credit, how much would I spend if I had to pay cash for it? _____

What does this tell me about my ability to purchase it on credit?

_____

❒ Which stores in my area might sell this product for less? _____

❏ Is the product or a similar one available by mail order at a lower price? If so, where? _____

❏ Is the mail-order price still lower when shipping and/or handling fees are added? _____

❏ If my area has high sales taxes, how much could I save if I purchase the product in a nearby area that has lower sales taxes? _____

❏ Could I benefit by joining a wholesale club that sells the product? If so, which club? _____

   Will I still come out ahead after I pay the membership fee? _____

❏ Is this product more expensive or in higher demand in my area than in other locations? If so, how much might I save if I were to buy it in another city or region? _____

❏ Could a discount buying service negotiate a lower price than I could get for this product? _____

❏ Could I obtain a display or demonstration model in great condition at a reduced price? _____

❏ Could I obtain a better deal if I purchased more than one product at a time, such as going in with friends to buy two or more? _____

❏ What are the pros and cons of spending more money now in order to get what I really want? Or waiting until later to buy? _____

✓ **Consider the Timing of Your Purchase.** Various items go on sale at different times of the year, and you can save big on major (and minor) purchases by using timing in your favor. The following questions will help you to determine the best (and worst) times to buy a particular product.

❏ Does this product go on sale periodically? Seasonally? _____

If so, how much lower is the sale price than the regular price? _____

❏ During sale time, will I be able to obtain the specific product I want, or will I have to choose from a limited selection or reduced inventory?
_____

❏ Can I wait to buy the product until it goes on sale? Why or why not?
_____

❏ If I buy the product at a sale time, what problems might I have to overcome (such as storage, unnecessary wear, fewer parts available, and so on)?
_____
_____

Remember the three items that you plan to purchase within the next year? Write a short shopping/buying strategy for each:

1. _____
_____
_____

2. _____
_____
_____

3. _____
_____
_____

✓ **Consider the Alternatives.** Buying a brand-new product may not be the only way to meet your needs. Sometimes a lower-cost alternative will do the job. Don't overlook these money-saving options:

❏ Would it be more economical and just as easy to rent or borrow this item instead of buying it? Why or why not? _____
_____

❏ Can I obtain a reliable, used product through the want ads? _____

❏ Where can I purchase a used product that will be suitable and have a good warranty/guarantee? _____

❏ How much will this option save me? _____

❏ How much might I save if I purchase a rebuilt product that has a strong warranty/guarantee? _____

Where could I find a reliable dealer for such a product? _____
_____

❏ How much will I save if I purchase a slightly damaged product that still has a good warranty/guarantee? _____

❏ Could I build or make a suitable product (perhaps with the help of friends or family), given my time and the cost of equipment and materials? If so, how much might I save? _____

✓ **Consider Optional Warranties or Extended Service.** Almost anything you buy today may come with an optional warranty or extended service agreement. In fact, Amanda recently bought a thirteen-dollar kitchen appliance and was asked if she would like to purchase an extended service agreement for four dollars!

❏ How much will the optional warranty or extended service cost? _____
_____

❏ How much does it really cover? _____
_____

❏ Will it cover the problems I am likely to have with this product? _____
Which significant, potential problems are excluded from coverage? _____
_____

❏ How long will the coverage last beyond the standard warranty? _____

❏ How much money could this coverage save me? _____
Is that amount of protection worth the cost? _____

❑ If I simply saved the amount I would pay for the extended warranty, will that money cover most of the cost of potential repairs? _____

❑ What do service technicians say about the warranty/guarantee in light of the product's repair history? _____

ADDITIONAL WAYS TO SAVE ON ITEMS LARGE AND SMALL

Consider Methods of Payment/Terms

Pay cash for purchases whenever possible. This will help you limit your share of consumer debt (discussed in the previous chapter). Occasionally you may need to buy an item on credit because of a possible cashshortage and a seeming one-time bargain that awaits. But a bargain may not be such a great bargain if you choose a high-cost method of payment. Here's how to determine if you really have the resources to make the purchase and to verify the real cost if you don't pay cash.

❑ If I must finance the purchase, how much will the financing cost me?

Cost Description:		Dollar Cost:
1. How much down payment is required?		$
2. How much are the monthly payments?	$	
3. How many monthly payments must I make?		
4. Total cost of monthly payments (multiply line 2 by line 3):		$
5. Total payment required (add lines 1 and 4):		$
6. Original cost of product:		$
7. Difference between original cost and actual amount to be paid (subtract line 6 from line 5):		$

❑ Do you still consider it worthwhile to finance the purchase? _____

❑ Whenever you finance a purchase, make sure you know the answers to these questions:
  ★ What is the interest rate being charged? _____
  ★ Is the lender giving me as good a rate as I could obtain elsewhere, such as at a bank or savings and loan? _____
  ★ What does the small print in the contract say? (Never sign anything you haven't completely read and understood.) _____
  _____

★ What changes in my future income might affect my ability to pay for this purchase? (New baby? Job loss? Surgery? Upcoming bills?) _____

_____

❐ If the product should prove defective or unsuitable for your use, can you return it for a cash refund or a store credit on another item? Will there be a "restocking" fee if you do? _____

Return Defective or Unused Merchandise

Unless you have to drive many miles and stand in line for hours, make it a practice to return unused items, new gifts that you'd like to exchange, and defective merchandise. (Even items that only cost five or ten dollars are worth returning.) If you don't have a receipt for the purchase and there's no identifiable store code on the item you wish to return, try calling the store manager and explaining your situation. Quite often he or she will at least allow a credit toward future purchases.

List the unused or defective items you have around the house (including those in the attic or garage) that could be returned: _____

Stock Up and Buy Ahead

Have you ever spent Christmas Eve trying to find a special gift, only to discover that stores had been sold out of what you wanted to buy for days? Ever run out of eggs you needed for a recipe that had to go into the oven in ten minutes? By stocking up on sale items and buying ahead, you can save money, time, and transportation costs. Sometimes spending money now can save you money later.

Consider the options you have for stocking up and buying ahead. Check each box for which you can answer "yes" to the question. Do you:

❐ Have adequate space (pantry, basement, or extra cupboards) in which to store items you buy before you need them?

❐ Have a freezer in which to store food?

❐ Have enough cash left after expenses to purchase items in bulk or well before you intend to use them?

❐ Tend to use the same products again and again?

❐ Regularly use seasonal items that you could purchase on sale at the end of one season and use the following season? (Consider clothing, outdoor gear, sporting equipment, school supplies, and so on.)

❐ Frequently buy basic gifts for family members and/or friends? (Consider wedding gifts, birthday gifts, Christmas gifts, and so on.)

If you checked most or all of the above boxes, chances are you can save quite a bit by making seasonal and gift purchases at the right times. To get started, complete the charts below. (We have given you a few ideas.) These charts can help you make wise advance purchases of gifts, food, and household supplies and clothing. Then begin the adventure of buying at the right time—for less!

GIFTS

Name or occasion	Gift idea(s)	When needed
Grandma	earrings, sweater, new novel by favorite author	Christmas
Wedding	coffeemaker, photo frames, glassware	May

FOOD/HOUSEHOLD: The determining factor in how much you can buy at any given time varies according to your individual needs and circumstances. At times, shelf life will limit the amount you can buy; at other times, storage space or financial resources will be the limiting factors.

Product	Shelf life	Most I can use during shelf life	Most I can store	Most I can afford to buy
Ground beef	4 months	6 lbs.	10 lbs.	4 lbs.
Paper towels	no limit		8 rolls	12 rolls
Canned fruit		20 cans	12 cans	10 cans

*When figuring shelf life, consider not only the maximum length of time allowed for safety/usability but the maximum length of time you want to store the product.

CLOTHING

Need for whom	What needed	When needed	Anticipated size when needed
Anna	Winter coat — prefer pink	October	6X
Dad	golf shoes	May	11 1/2

Make additional charts as needed for your future purchases. It may be helpful to chart your needs for such items as yard care products, tools, sports equipment, or pet care products (especially if you have pets, such as horses, that eat a lot).

In addition, stock up during store sales. Even though everyone knows that stores have periodic sales, people are often not willing to wait or don't plan ahead to determine what their needs will be. Try to anticipate what you'll need ahead of time. If an item you need goes on sale, and you can afford the purchase, buy it now. If you plan to replace an item, try to make it last until the stores have sales.

Here are just some of the items to look for when considering a sale. (For a more detailed checklist on evaluating the value of sales items, we recommend *Living Smart, Spending Less,* page 55). The next time you're ready to shop at a sale, review the following checklist before leaving home. Then you'll have an even better chance of finding what you need and feeling great after your purchase!

❒ Is the sale price really a good price? (Perhaps prices are always cheaper at competing stores.)

❒ How do the sale items compare in quality to similar items in another store?

❒ Has other merchandise been substituted for the advertised merchandise?

❒ Are only a few items sale priced, just to get you into the store?

❒ Which guarantees, return policy, or warranty will you receive on a given item? (Always consider the risk of "all sales are final" sales.)

With a little practice and observation, you may be able to improve your "sales savvy."

Take Up the Shopping Challenge—Today!

Start applying these tips today, building on the shopping skills you already have. Paying the lowest prices for the products you need or want will make a big difference to your bottom line!

4
Choosing a Place to Live

Today, housing choices abound. Barbara rents a house with several roommates. Patrick, who just graduated from college, is renting a small apartment until he pays off school debts and earns a higher salary. Marcie, an urban professional, thinks buying a condominium is "the only way to go." Her brother and sister-in-law, however, just bought a home in the suburbs.

Perhaps you are renting until you can save enough money to buy a home. Or you may be renting because the financial commitment and responsibility of home ownership would interfere with your personal goals or priorities. Perhaps you are in the position of having saved or inherited enough money to choose whether you will buy or rent a place to live.

DETERMINE YOUR HOUSING REQUIREMENTS CAREFULLY

Whether you plan to rent or buy your home, you'd be wise to make an informed decision on your housing situation. By asking the right questions and following basic guidelines to determine your housing requirements, you can save quite a bit of money on housing costs while enhancing your lifestyle. And you may avoid making a regrettable housing decision that could prove to be expensive.

As you complete the following charts, carefully think through your current and future housing needs. Doing so will help you become aware of the requirements—or strong preferences—your living space must meet. The more honest you are now, with yourself and/or a spouse or friend, the better decisions you will make. Feel free to add your personal requirements to these charts and to make copies as needed.

Interior Requirements Chart

Type of overall layout preferred:	
Minimum space required:	_____ square feet
Number and size of bedroom(s) needed:	
Bedroom location(s) needed:	
Kitchen size and layout preferred:	
Other kitchen preferences:	Gas or electric? Updated or older?
Specific bathroom preferences: Size:	
Number of bathrooms needed:	
Other bathroom features:	
Updated or older?	
Other room preferences and sizes:	Family room, living room, or great room?
Formal dining room?	
Study?	
Home office?	
Media room?	
Garage/carport required?	No Yes
Size preferred:	
How much closet storage needed?	Lots Some Little
Other requirements:	
Type of closets preferred:	
Type of flooring preferred:	
Type of heating preferred:	Wood F/A Gas Oil Solar Hot Water Electric Propane
Fireplace or stove preferred:	Gas Wood Not needed
Special electrical outlets needed:	How many? _____ Where?
Laundry facilities needed?	No Yes
Particular view preferred?	No Yes
Central air conditioning required?	No Yes
Basement needed?	No Yes

Exterior Requirements Chart

Yard size preferred:	
Yard features:	Large lawn?
Garden space?	
Dog run?	
Mature trees?	
Sprinkler system?	
Fencing?	
Outdoor living preferences:	Privacy?
Child's play area?	
Deck or patio?	
Storage needed for outdoor and sports equipment:	
Exterior maintenance:	High Moderate Low
Special access requirements:	

Location Requirements Chart

The adage says, "Three things are most important when buying a home: location, location, and location." That is true not only from an investment perspective but also from a personal viewpoint. Will the home you're considering be a suitable and pleasant place in which to live? The following chart will help you evaluate your needs and preferences. There is room to write additional information at the bottom of the chart.

Preferred setting:	Urban? Rural? Suburban? Country club community? Restricted access community? Other? _____
Neighborhood preferences:	Historic? Well-established? New? Quiet? Residential? Mixed residential and business?
Character of neighborhood:	Young families? Retirees? Established families? Singles? Friendly? Close-knit? Aloof?

Type of housing in neighborhood:	Single-family? Multi-family? Are most homes owner or tenant occupied?
Neighborhood condition:	Well-kept? Safe? In transition (many "for sale" signs)?
Neighborhood value:	Is it appreciating or depreciating? Are homes of similar or greatly varied value? What has been the resale value history?
Proximity to facilities, services, and special people:	Distance/time to work: Distance/time to school: Distance/time to airport: Distance/time to church: Distance/time to hospital: Distance/time to recreation: Distance to family/friends:
Local services:	Is snow plowed for you? Is there garbage service? Is public transportation available? Is there quality police and fire protection? Other? _____
Local schools:	Are public schools high quality? Are private schools high quality? Do you know and like the school(s) your child(ren) will attend?
Local rules and regulations:	Tight zoning laws? Strict covenants? Adequate parking?

Utility and Maintenance Requirements

Regardless of whether you rent or buy, you would be wise to determine ahead of time the cost of utilities. Inspecting previous utility bills will tell you a great deal about the place in which you may live. You don't want to move in and discover that you can't afford to pay the bills during the coldest and/or warmest months of the year. If possible, ask to review several recent summer (air conditioning) bills and several recent winter (heating) bills and then determine what the "average" bill is likely to be for each of the appropriate categories. Renters who are offered free heat for a higher monthly rental payment may find that it's a worthwhile deal.

Utility Used:	Average Summer:	Average Winter:	Annual:
Natural gas	$	$	$
Oil	$	$	$
Propane	$	$	$
Electricity	$	$	$
Water	$	$	$
Sewer	$	$	$
Telephone (basic charge)	$	$	$
Other _____	$	$	$

TO RENT OR BUY: THAT IS THE QUESTION

Should you rent or buy your living space? The answer depends on many personal factors. You and/or your spouse or family can save a great deal of money by asking basic questions about your lifestyle and goals that will help clarify which option suits you best. If you plan to live in an area for only a few months, you probably want to rent instead of buy. If you travel extensively, a condominium or townhome community may provide better security than a home in the country. The following statements, questions, and checklists will help you clarify your thoughts so you can make the best choice.

Determine Your Needs

I plan to remain in the area _____ months _____ years.

I anticipate the following lifestyle change(s):
- ❏ _____ additional child(ren) in the home
- ❏ Going back to school full-time
- ❏ Changing jobs/careers
- ❏ Retiring
- ❏ Other: _____

I travel _____ days a week or _____ months a year.

I ❏ enjoy ❏ don't enjoy doing home and yard maintenance.

I have the following requirements that a landlord/manager might not want to or be able to accommodate (pets, hobbies, business needs, access):

_____

_____

_____

_____

I ❑ could ❑ could not   live with the restrictions most landlords/managers place on tenants.

I ❑ could ❑ could not   live with the inconveniences of having close neighbors (such as in an apartment).

I ❑ am ready to put down permanent roots ❑ want mobility.

Consider Creative Housing Options

Remember, renting an apartment or buying a single-family home are not the only housing options available. Check which of the following options might work for you.

❑ I could do maintenance work in exchange for a place to live.

❑ I could rent an apartment or a house with friends or family.

❑ I could live temporarily in a camper or recreational trailer at a campground, trailer park, or other site.

❑ I could do long-term housesitting for people who regularly leave their homes for two to six months at a time.

❑ I could, with the assistance of friends and/or subcontractors, build a new home or fix up an existing home.

Carefully Evaluate Your Financial Situation

Obviously finances play a key role in the type of housing you will choose. It is imperative that you determine how much you can afford to spend on housing before you buy. Generally a lender will allow your monthly mortgage payment and other housing expenses (insurance, taxes, interest) to total no more than 29 percent of your monthly gross income.[1] The lender will also add up all your debt obligations to see if the total is more than 41 percent of your gross income. If you have assets you could sell quickly to cover mortgage payments and have low consumer debt, a lender might give you a few extra percentage points. However, you ultimately must decide whether or not you can afford to repay a mortgage for the maximum qualifying amount.

Know Your Credit History

Your credit history will come into play when qualifying for a mortgage, so it's wise to have answers to the following:

What is your credit rating? _____

Is your credit history correct? If not, what must you do to correct it?

_____

What credit problems have you had within the past three to seven years?

_____

Have you changed career fields within the past three years? _____

Make Sure You Understand Your Ability to Repay the Loan

There's more to consider when buying a home than just what your monthly mortgage will cost. Thoroughly discuss your needs with a knowledgeable accountant and/or a Realtor, then complete the following checklist:

❑ I can make a down payment of at least $ _____.

❑ I can afford to pay closing costs of $ _____.

❑ I can qualify for a mortgage loan of $ _____with a monthly payment of $ _____. This means I need a loan rate less than _____ percent and a loan with the following terms: _____.

❑ I can live comfortably using the income remaining after my mortgage is paid.

❑ I think I'll be employed at my same job(s) for another year.

❑ I will be able to pay for each of the following:

_____ tax payments   _____ routine maintenance costs

_____ insurance payments   _____ building or community fees

❑ I have demonstrated that I can set aside money regularly that could be used for house payments.

IF YOU DECIDE TO BUY A HOME

For most people, buying a home is the investment of a lifetime. They will gain privacy and shelter. They also will have the opportunity to build equity, as their payments help them buy ownership in real estate. Therefore, making the right choice is critical because you have to live with what you buy, and buying the wrong house can cost you lots of money. So it's important to review your needs and finances, consider all options, and seek out the best help available.

The Final Exam

You've completed the worksheets presented earlier in the chapter. Now here's a "final exam," a summary evaluation of why you want or need a home and how you will pay for it.

Summarize your reasons

After considering all of your options, on a separate sheet of paper describe the home you want to buy (include type of home, size, number of rooms, special features, and condition):

Describe the optimum neighborhood and location for this home: _____

_____

_____

Why do you want to buy at this particular time? _____

_____

Is this a good time to buy? Why or why not? _____

_____

If it is not a good time to buy, do you have a compelling need to buy now, or could you wait for a better time to buy? _____

_____

Is it likely that you will find a better buy if you wait? _____

How long might you need to wait for the market to change? _____

Summarize your finances

How large a down payment are you able to make? _____

How much are you "prequalified" to borrow? _____

What is the monthly payment on this amount? _____

What is the maximum price you can pay for a home? _____

Sometimes the maximum amount for which you qualify isn't ideal for you. You may want to buy a lower-priced home that requires a lower monthly payment.

What monthly payment do you think is ideal for you? _____

Given the down payment you plan to make, and your ideal payment, what is the ideal price you can pay for a home? _____

Find a Competent Realtor

If you are comfortable with the answers, especially concerning your finances and the timing of a home purchase, you've passed your final exam. Now it's time to find a good Realtor who can answer further questions and help you purchase the right home.

Keep in mind that many Realtors work for the seller, not for you—the buyer. In contrast to this seller's agent, a buyer's agent works solely on your (buyer's) behalf, and a dual agent works on behalf of both the buyer and the seller. We recommend that you use a buyer's agent. (Turn to page 72 of *Living Smart, Spending Less* for a further discussion.)

Since you will spend quite a bit of time with your agent and since he or she can make a significant difference in the property you find and how much money you spend to purchase it, it's important to find a good agent. The following questions will help you in this process:

	YES	NO
Is the agent a licensed Realtor, in good standing with the local Board of Realtors?		
Does he/she know the local area well?		
Is the agent's company well established and well respected?		
Is the agent friendly and pleasant to be with?		
Does he/she show you properties that fit your requirements?		
Is the agent willing to show you government "repos"? If so, will he/she handle all the paperwork of such a purchase?		
Will the agent enthusiastically take your "low" offers to sellers? (By law he/she may be required to present all offers, but attitude can be important.)		
Does the agent really add insight to your observations about a home? Is he/she a good sounding board, helping you to distill information and make good decisions?		
Has anyone filed a formal complaint against the agent or agent's company with the Better Business Bureau, Board of Realtors, or state real estate commission?		

WHEN YOU FIND THE HOME YOU'D LIKE TO BUY

Once you have found the ideal home and are ready to make an offer on it, consider two key areas: the taxes/insurance costs and any maintenance problems that exist.

Evaluate the Taxes/Insurance You'll Have to Pay

The taxes for even a small home in an expensive area can cost a great deal. Before you buy a particular home, consider how much the taxes and property insurance will be. (Check with the county assessor's office to find out about any "hidden" or upcoming assessments.)

Annual insurance costs (structure)	$ _____
Annual insurance costs (belongings)	$ _____
Annual taxes	$ _____
When next assessment will be:	_____
Sum of annual taxes/insurance:	$ _____

Detect Any and All Maintenance Problems

By observing maintenance problems now, you will save money and avoid hassles later. Sometimes the seller will reduce the asking price when problems are brought to his/her attention. We suggest that you hire a home inspector to carefully inspect all aspects of the home you'd like to buy. (You may offer a contract based on the home passing such an inspection.) Whether or not you hire an inspector, watch for problems in the following areas. When you notice them, determine if you can do the repair work or if you'll have to hire a professional. Then receive written estimates for the repairs.

Home Inspection Checklist	Action/Estimated Cost:
Site Problems	
Potential flooding, erosion	
Diseased or dead trees	
Overgrown plantings near house	
Building Problems	
Worn shingles	
Leaky gutters	
Stovepipe/chimney repairs needed	
Siding in poor condition	
Porches/sidewalks/decks that need repair	

Exterior doors that don't seal well	
Structural Problems	
Floors sagging, creaking, uneven	
Doors/windows don't fit well	
Water stains on walls/ceilings	
Cracks in walls/ceilings	
Cracks/settling of foundation/walls	
Signs of termite/insect damage	
Health Hazards	
Asbestos	
Lead-based paint	
Contaminated water system	
Heating/Cooling	
Insufficient insulation	
Inefficient/inadequate heating system	
Inefficient/inadequate air conditioning	
Inefficient doors/windows	
Caulking/weatherstripping needed	
Sewer/Water System	
Sewer backs up	
Septic tank clogged up	
Leach field smells/has holes or pools	
Water pressure is too low	
Plumbing fixtures need repair	
Inefficient/inadequate hot water heater	
Electricity	
Not up to current code	
Inadequate interior lighting	
Inadequate outlets/switches	
Other Warning Signs	
Appliances to remain in the house aren't in good repair	
Bad odors in room(s)	
Stained carpet	
Walls/ceilings need paint	

Other repairs needed (if any):

1. _____
2. _____
3. _____

Negotiate and Prepare the Contract Carefully

When it's time for you and your agent to negotiate details with the seller and carefully draw up a contract, the more attention you pay to the negotiating process the more likely you are to save money and end up with a deal you can live with. (In some states, Realtors must use real estate commission-approved contracts, which decreases the likelihood of a poor contract being drawn up.)

Use this checklist to ensure that the following items are included in your offer. Whenever possible, go over details with a real estate attorney who can point out problem areas in the offer/contract. This is especially important if the real estate deal is complicated.

❑ A legal description of the property.

❑ A list of all items to be sold with the home—window coverings, air conditioners, appliances that are not built in, storage shed, etc.—and their model and serial numbers, when appropriate.

❑ How much earnest money you will put down, and which third party will hold that deposit.

❑ The price you are willing to pay. (Be prepared to negotiate.)

❑ The conditions that will void your offer without penalizing you. Typically these include: obtaining satisfactory financing, selling an existing home by a certain date, and/or favorable inspections.

❑ A list of everything the present owner agrees to fix before you buy the home, along with all terms and conditions contained in the original offer.

❑ When you will take possession of the home.

❑ Who pays which closing costs.

Shop for the Best Mortgage Loan

Interest rates are fickle. Like a roller-coaster ride, there are pleasant surprises when they dip, but uncertainty (and anxiety) await when they climb. But whether mortgage interest rates are high or low, they can vary from lender to lender, so it is wise to shop around. After all, paying a mortgage every month takes a chunk out of your spending plan. Use the following checklist and consult with your Realtor and/or accountant to determine the options that will be best for you.

✓ Shop for the best interest rates. Even a fraction of a percentage point could save you thousands of dollars during the life of your loan! For example, if you borrow $100,000 using a fixed-rate, thirty-year loan, obtaining the financing at 9 percent instead of 9 1/4 percent will save you $28,859 during the thirty years.)

✓ Evaluate the kinds of available loans. Common mortgage options include a conventional fixed-rate, adjustable-rate, graduated-payment, or balloon. Learn the differences—and the benefits and drawbacks—of each type.

List the reputable lenders that provide the lowest interest rates for the type of loan that is best for you.

Lender:	Type/Length of Loan:	Interest Rate:	Monthly Payment:	Total Cost of Loan:

✓ To evaluate the specific offerings of the above lenders, consider all aspects of the loan. Here are ten questions you should ask before settling on the mortgage lender and type of loan:

❑ Yes ❑ No   Will the lender charge me "points" at closing? If so, how many?

❑ Yes ❑ No   Have I received a list of other closing costs? How much will the total be?

❑ Yes ❑ No   Can I afford a shorter-term loan? (That would increase the size of the monthly payment, but it would allow you to build equity faster and dramatically reduce the amount of interest you will pay.)

❑ Yes ❑ No   Do I know how large a down payment will be required?

❑ Yes ❑ No   Do I want to consider an adjustable-rate mortgage, which offers a low interest rate that will later go up? If so, how high can the interest rate go? Which indicator serves as the basis on which the rate is determined?

❑ Yes ❑ No   Can I pay off the mortgage in advance without a penalty?

❑ Yes ❑ No   Can I make my own property tax and insurance-premium payments instead of having those funds held in escrow?

❑ Yes ❑ No   Does the lender want to be able to force me to repay or refinance the loan at any time? If so, find another lender.

❑ Yes ❑ No   If I choose to "lock in" my interest rate before I close on my home, will the fee be reasonable? How much will it be, and when will the "lock" expire? (Some lenders will credit the "lock in" fee toward the mortgage origination fee.)

❑ Yes ❑ No   Can I assume an existing loan with a lower rate without the interest rate increasing?

IF YOU DECIDE TO RENT

Your housing requirements may make renting more practical than buying a home. If so, you'll need to evaluate various leases that are commonly used in the rental of apartments and homes. Read each lease fully and carefully before making your final decision. If you don't understand a lease completely, don't sign it until your questions are answered satisfactorily. Find someone who can explain the lease to you or pay a lawyer to read it. Perhaps a local housing official can advise you.

As you go through this checklist, make sure the lease you sign addresses each relevant point. Otherwise, you may be required to pay more money than you originally planned.

Terms of occupancy:

    Rental unit's location: _____

    Dates of my occupancy: _____

    Security deposit? ❑ No ❑ Yes : $_____

    Terms for return of deposit: _____

Rental payment terms:

    Rent due each month: _____

    Date rent is due: _____

    Is there a grace period? ❑ No ❑ Yes: _____ days

    Are late charges required? ❑ No ❑ Yes: _____ dollars

    How long will the lease last? ❑ 1 year ❑ 6 months ❑ _____

    May the rent increase? ❑ No ❑ Yes

    By how much? $_____ How often? _____

    Is there a lease renewal option? ❑ No ❑ Yes

At what rent? $_____ At what terms? ❑ Monthly ❑ _____

Utilities:
Which utilities are included in the lease payment?
❑ Water ❑ Sewer ❑ Heat ❑ Electricity ❑ Gas
❑ Propane ❑ Trash
Will I share utility costs with another tenant? ❑ No ❑ Yes

Lease Restrictions and Inclusions

Make sure you understand and can abide by all of the rules, restrictions, and obligations associated with your lease. Things to check on include (but are not limited to): (1) storage regulations; (2) regulations for children or pets; (3) your ability to sublet if you move before the lease is up, and the terms under which it is permitted; (4) the number of people who can live in the unit; (5) rules/regulations for use of public areas such as the pool, laundry area, or parking lot; (6) your ability to work or have a business at home.

Provisions for maintenance may be stipulated in the lease. Check for the following in any lease you are considering:

❑ Snow removal ❑ Lawn care ❑ Other: _____

❑ Yes ❑ No   The landlord/manager will agree in writing to fix any existing or future maintenance problem(s) with rental unit.

❑ Yes ❑ No   The landlord will agree in writing to perform or bear costs for cleaning, general upkeep, and appliance repair.

❑ Yes ❑ No   I will receive advance warning before the manager/landlord enters my unit.

❑ Yes ❑ No   Parking facilities are provided. (Available at extra cost?)

FINAL CONSIDERATIONS BEFORE SIGNING THE LEASE

Before signing a lease, be sure you can answer each of these questions with a no. Otherwise, you will need to take the actions indicated before signing.

❑ Yes ❑ No   Are there any clauses I can't live with?
If yes, will landlord/manager cross it/them off the contract and initial and date the change(s)?

❑ Yes ❑ No   Are there any problems with the apartment?
If yes, make a dated list of all the problems and have the landlord/manager sign the list. If he or she refuses and you still

want to rent the unit, take photos of the problems and send a certified copy of the list to the landlord/manager.

❑ Yes ❑ No   Are there any blank spaces in the lease?

If yes, fill in the blanks correctly.

❑ Yes ❑ No   Are there any changes to the lease?

If yes, both you and the landlord/manager must sign and date them. If the changes will not fit on the lease, create an addendum to the lease and write on the lease that all parties agree to the attached and signed addendum.

1. *A Home of Your Own: Helpful Advice from HUD on Choosing, Buying, and Enjoying a Home.* U.S. Department of Housing and Urban Development, Washington, DC 20410, May 1991.

5
Save Money in All Corners—Reduce Your Home Energy Costs

Whether you live in a new, energy-efficient home or an older, drafty one, most likely the cost of living in it is your greatest monthly expense. In addition to mortgage or rent payments, you face ever-increasing utility costs (unless all utility costs are included in your rent). If you take steps to reduce your utility usage, however, you can come out many after-tax dollars ahead—and use that extra cash in more profitable ways.

As a homeowner or apartment dweller, you will save money by implementing the tips that apply to your situation. Some of them require virtually no time or energy, such as turning off unnecessary lights and using the right-sized pan on the range top. Others require ten to fifteen minutes of your time—or hours of commitment.

Don't be afraid to try some of these suggestions, even if you don't consider yourself to be handy around the house. They can lead to major savings in four areas of energy use: water, electricity, cooling, and heating. Energy-saving projects can be fun and innovative, and you can learn many basic repairs. Experiment and see what works for you given your time, finances, and other constraints.

REDUCE YOUR WATER BILL

Outdoor Water Use

Summertime can be draining on lawns and gardens as well as people. Unless you live in the Pacific Northwest or other moist areas where gentle rains keep things green almost year-around, you may be using a large amount of clean, drinkable water to keep your lawn, flowers, and trees healthy. Put a check mark next to each of the following tips that would help to conserve water, reduce your water bill, and possibly improve the health of your yard and garden, too.

- ❑ Place mulch around well-established trees, shrubs, and flowers to help the soil retain moisture and retard weed growth.
- ❑ Use natural landscaping that requires little water.
- ❑ Control your family's outdoor use of water, particularly when washing the car or playing in the sprinklers.
- ❑ Cover the swimming pool or spa to slow evaporation.
- ❑ Water your garden or lawn early in the morning or late in the evening when the water will not evaporate as quickly.
- ❑ Adjust sprinklers so they water only your lawn and flowers, not the street or driveway.
- ❑ Promptly repair leaks in your in-ground sprinkler system.
- ❑ Water the lawn and garden more thoroughly and less frequently.
- ❑ Use a soaker hose instead of a sprinkler to water your garden.
- ❑ Let your grass grow a little taller during hot months to increase moisture retention and protect the roots.

Indoor Water Use

Did you know that a leaky faucet could cost you as much as fifty dollars a year? Or that the installation of an inexpensive flow restrictor in the shower head could save a family of four an average of 1,600 gallons of water monthly?[1] So take a hard look at how to save on your indoor water use.

Are you allowing your hard-earned money to drip down the drain from leaky faucets? Take a leaky faucet inventory and list below any faucets that drip. Then schedule a time to fix them! (While you're checking for leaks, check also for toilets that don't stop running.)

_____

_____

Test your water-saving savvy! Check off the water-saving tips you practice or could put to use. Then add your favorite indoor water savers to the list.

- ❑ Put only as much water into the tub as you need.
- ❑ Install an inexpensive flow restrictor in the shower head or a combination flow restrictor/aerator.
- ❑ Don't run the water constantly while you brush your teeth or shave. Turn it on

and off as you need it.
- ❑ Take brief showers instead of baths and turn off the water while you lather up.
- ❑ If you need to run tap water until it's the right temperature, catch the excess water in a jug and use it for other purposes. (One friend uses it to water his plants.)
- ❑ Wash fruits or vegetables over a pan or bucket and use the dirty water on indoor plants or in the garden.
- ❑ Refrigerate a pitcher of water so you don't have to run the tap every time you want a cool drink.
- ❑ _____
- ❑ _____
- ❑ _____

Consider replacing an older toilet with a new one that requires less water. How does the cost of operating the existing toilet compare to the cost of installing and operating a new toilet?_____

_____

HEATING WATER

Heating water is expensive and may account for 20 percent or more of your utility costs. It isn't as hard as you may think to slash the cost of heating water. Start planning your money-saving strategy today.

Minimize the Cost of Heating Water

Think carefully about the money-saving options below and determine which steps you can take now and which ones you would like to do when time or finances allow. Just see how much you can save!

Do When?	Cost?

Money Saver:

✓ Turn down the water heater thermostat. For every ten-degree reduction, you'll save more than 6 percent in water heating energy.[2] Start at 120 or 125 degrees unless you own a dishwasher that requires a higher temperature. A lower temperature setting can also make scalding less likely.

✓ If you leave home for longer than a weekend, turn the storage water heater down or off. If it has a pilot light, be sure you know how to relight it safely.

Do When?	Cost?

✓ Install a programmable timer so your storage water heater will only heat water when you need it and/or when electric rates are lower. Be sure the timer matches the requirements of your water heater.

✓ Make sure the water heater is the right size for your use. If it's too large, energy will be wasted in keeping excess water warm; if it's too small, energy will be wasted in quickly heating incoming water.

✓ Consider replacing an inefficient water heater with one that has a high Energy Efficiency Ratio. Even if you pay more up front, a high-efficiency model will save you money year after year. Some utility companies offer rebates when you upgrade to a high-efficiency unit.

✓ Raise the temperature of the water entering the storage water heater by adding a storage tank in which the cold water can warm up before entering the water heater.

✓ Consider installing a do-it-yourself or ready-made solar water heater.

✓ Install a fiberglass insulation "blanket" around the basement storage water heater to cut your water heating bills up to 9 percent.

Minimize the Waste of Heated Water

Once water is heated, the way you use it can either cost you money or help you save it. Do you:

❏ Turn down the hot water instead of turning up the cold water when you want to cool the temperature of water coming from the tap?

❏ Select cold/cold or warm/cold instead of hot water cycles when you wash clothes? (If necessary, let clothing agitate longer to get it clean.)

❏ Run cold water rather than hot water into the garbage disposer?

❏ Always load your dishwasher properly and run it only when it is full? The typical dishwasher uses fourteen gallons of hot water per load,[3] so don't use it more than you need to.

❏ Use the "rinse hold" cycle cautiously? It uses three to seven gallons of hot water each time you run it.[4] If needed, manually presoak dishes that have cheese, hardened rice, or other food substances on them.

In what other ways can you minimize your use of heated water or use it more efficiently? (Insulate hot water pipes? Install a "demand" hot water heater?)

SAVE ELECTRICITY (OR NATURAL GAS)

After we moved into our current home, we declared war on the high electric bills paid by the previous residents. Within a few months, we had reduced our electric usage by nearly 50 percent. (This included substantial savings achieved by upgrading the electric hot water heater.)

We've emphasized electricity savings, but if you use natural gas, the same guidelines often apply. By applying tips appropriate to your situation, you may be able to reduce your electric or gas bills by one-third or more.

SAVING ENERGY IN THE LAUNDRY ROOM

Washing machines, gas or electric clothes dryers, and irons consume a significant amount of energy—and money. Check off the following energy savers that you regularly practice.

❏ Iron clothes that require the lowest amount of heat first, then work on higher temperature fabrics as the iron heats up.

❏ Remove clothes that need ironing from the dryer when they're still damp and iron them immediately.

❏ Whenever possible, buy no-iron clothing.

❏ Use an indoor and/or outdoor clothesline instead of a dryer whenever possible. (Doing so during the summer months could save you about sixty-five dollars a year.[5])

❏ When using a clothes dryer, place items of similar thickness in each load. (Two heavy towels added to a load of lightweight shirts will increase the drying time for the whole load.)

❏ Don't put too many items into one dryer load; that lengthens drying time.

❏ Dry clothing in consecutive loads. A warmed-up dryer requires less energy than a cool dryer.

❏ Keep the lint screen and outside exhaust vent of the dryer clean so air flow is not limited.

❏ Run full instead of partial washing machine loads, but don't overload the washer.

❏ Clean the washing machine's lint filter after each use.

Which energy savers will you begin to use on a regular basis? _____

SAVING ENERGY IN THE KITCHEN

A typical kitchen has more appliances than any other room, and some of them are major energy consumers. The questions that follow will help you conduct your own kitchen energy audit. See how many ways you can cut down on kitchen energy costs. (For more tips, read *Living Smart, spending Less.*)

The Range and Oven

For which uses would it be more efficient to use a microwave, crockpot (slow cooker), or toaster oven rather than your range or oven? _____
_____
_____

How long do you preheat the oven or broiler? (Eight to ten minutes should be long enough.) _____

Now test yourself on your everyday energy-saving habits. How often do you:

	Always	Sometimes	Never
◆ Match the size of the range's heating element or flame to the pan? (A small pan on a large burner wastes energy.)			
◆ Turn off the range or oven when food is nearly cooked and let residual heat finish the cooking?			
◆ Use pots and pans that have flat bottoms and tightly fitting covers?			
◆ Turn on the range when the pan is on the burner, not before?			
◆ Keep burner reflectors and range-top burners clean so they will reflect heat more efficiently?			
◆ Use a timer instead of peeking in on your food? Every time you open the oven door, you lose as much as 20 percent of the heat![6]			
◆ Bake in the evenings during the summer to reduce cooling costs?			
◆ Cook several food items in the oven at the same time?			

How did you do? If you answered *Always* to nearly all of the questions on the previous page, congratulations! If not, there's room for improvement. Start making several of these energy-saving habits a part of your daily routine today.

Did you know . . . that a gas oven or range with electronic ignition instead of pilot lights can save you money? You can save up to a third of your gas use—53 percent on the top burners and 41 percent in the oven.[7]

The Freezer and Refrigerator

A freezer or refrigerator can use quite a bit of electricity, but you may be able to reduce the cost by conducting your own efficiency check and using the appliance efficiently.

Freezer/Refrigerator Efficiency Check:

❑ Stick a dollar bill between the door gasket and the frame. If it pulls out easily, the door seals needs to be repaired or replaced. Also watch for frost or condensation along the door's edge.

❑ Position the refrigerator or freezer where air circulation is good so the heated air can escape from the coils. Also keep the unit away from heat sources (oven, direct sunlight, and so on).

❑ Adjust the thermostat.

✓ The inside temperature of a refrigerator should be between thirty-four and thirty-eight degrees Fahrenheit.

✓ For long-term freezer storage, the thermostat should be set to zero degrees Fahrenheit. There is no need to set it colder.

❑ Check the frost level on manual-defrost models and defrost before the ice is 1/4 inch thick. (Frost buildup causes the unit to work harder and consume more power to maintain temperature.)

❑ If your unit has a power-saver switch, is it set properly? Always follow the manufacturer's instructions.

❑ When was the last time you cleaned underneath and behind the unit? Dust and dirt can reduce air circulation, reducing the effectiveness of the motor and coils. (Unplug the unit while you clean it, and be sure to plug it back in again when you are finished.)

❑ If your refrigerator or freezer is fifteen years old or older, you may benefit by buying a more recent, more efficient model. You may recoup your expense in just a few years, particularly if your area has high electric rates.

✓ Also consider buying a chest freezer, which doesn't allow as much cold air to escape as an upright does.

✓ Keep in mind that a frost-free unit requires up to 35 percent more energy to operate than a manual defrost unit.

What conclusions or changes will you make as a result of your efficiency check?

_____

_____

_____

No matter how efficient your refrigerator or freezer is, the way in which you use it on a daily basis makes a difference in the overall energy cost. Test yourself on your energy-savings habits. Do you:

	Always	Sometimes	Never
☞ Open the refrigerator or freezer as seldom as possible?			
☞ Allow warm foods to cool down a bit before putting them into the refrigerator or freezer? (Don't leave them out too long!)			
☞ Keep the freezer as full as possible? The cold mass helps to retain cold. If you can't afford or don't need that much food, gradually fill the freezer with plastic jugs of water.			
☞ Place large quantities of food into the freezer gradually? If you put in too much food at once, the motor could overheat or the food could spoil if it freezes too slowly.			
☞ Cover liquids and foods in a frost-free unit? Otherwise moisture that evaporates will cause the unit to use more energy.			

How did you do? If you answered *Always* to nearly all of the questions above, congratulations! If not, there's room for improvement. List at least three energy-saving habits that you will make a part of your daily routine.

_____

_____

_____

_____

The Dishwasher and Other Kitchen Gadgets

Many renters and homeowners have dishwashers. Because the dishwasher and other kitchen conveniences can cost you when the electric bill comes due, begin to use certain energy-saving practices.

Which energy-saving cycles does your dishwasher have? _____

How frequently do you use those features? _____

If your dishwasher doesn't have energy-saving cycles, you can open the unit before the drying cycle starts and air dry the dishes, saving as much as 10 percent of the electricity used. This also adds heat and humidity to your home, which can be particularly beneficial during winter months.

Do you air dry your dishes? Why or why not? _____

Count the number of electric-powered, small kitchen appliances and gadgets you have: _____

How many of them are really necessary or are well-suited to your present needs? (For example, do you really need a four-slot toaster, or will a two-slot model serve you better?) _____

Which ones could you live without? _____

Suggestion for future savings: Focus on buying energy-efficient electrical gadgets that you need, rather than those that corporate marketers dreamed up.

SAVING ENERGY WITH OTHER HOUSEHOLD APPLIANCES

Other household appliances can add more to your overall energy costs than you might think. Go through your home room by room and note the high-energy appliances you use. Record each one on the chart below and write down what you can do to minimize the energy consumption of that appliance. Some examples are already listed.

Appliance:	How to save energy:
Vacuum cleaner	Empty bags before they become overloaded.
Heated waterbed (a high-energy user)	Use a timer so it won't heat the water unnecessarily. Consider buying a conventional bed.
Portable electric heater	Use sparingly. Most are not designed for constant use, and they use lots of electricity.

Motor-driven equipment (such as a table saw)	*Let the motor run continuously instead of turning it on and off between cuts because most of the electricity is used to get the motor started.*

DON'T BE IN THE DARK ABOUT LIGHTING SAVINGS

You can do many things to reduce lighting costs. Most of them don't cost much and are easy to do.

Brighten Up Without Artificial Light

Light-colored paint, carpeting, window coverings, and upholstery can dramatically reduce the amount of light needed in a room. White reflects 80 percent of light, beige 66 percent, and peach 53 percent.[8]

How could you brighten up the interior of your home by making different choices in paint, carpeting, window coverings, or upholstery? _____

_____

_____

In what ways could you brighten the interior of your home by using natural light more effectively (such as opening shades and curtains or installing a skylight)?_____

_____

_____

Money-Saving Tips for Artificial Light

Did you know that you can save energy simply by changing light bulbs? You can! Consider the following tips, and then place a check mark in front of those you can use in the future.

❑ Use a high-wattage bulb instead of several low-wattage bulbs that add up to the same wattage. The high-wattage bulb gives out more lumens per watt than the low-wattage bulbs.

❏ Experiment to see where you can replace high-wattage bulbs with low-wattage bulbs and still have adequate light.

❏ Whenever possible, use fluorescent lamps instead of incandescent bulbs. Although they are more expensive to buy, fluorescent bulbs provide more lumens per watt, last up to ten times as long, and work well in areas where lights are not frequently turned on and off.

❏ Unless a fixture is hard to reach, use inexpensive, regular light bulbs instead of expensive, long-life bulbs that use more energy.

❏ Take unneeded light bulbs out of multiple-bulb fixtures and replace them with burned-out ones. Or partially unscrew unneeded bulbs. (Having no bulb in a socket can be dangerous.)

❏ Clean lighting fixtures, especially the surfaces of light bulbs and fluorescent tubes. Dirt blocks light.

❏ Use solid-state dimmers on incandescent lamps so you can choose exactly how much light you want. (Rheostat-type dimmers, on the other hand, use a large amount of electricity while dimming.)

❏ Use clear light bulbs. (They produce more light than frosted ones.)

MONITOR YOUR ELECTRICITY USAGE AND BENEFITS

It pays to make sure that you do not spend any more than you need to for electricity. It's also helpful to know which services and resources are available from your electric company. Believe it or not, your electric company can help you save money!

Monitor Your Billing

Learn to read your electric meter so you can compute your electricity usage. Read the meter from left to right and always use the lower number if the arrow is between numbers. Since the number of kilowatt-hours you use is cumulative, subtract your earlier readings from later readings.

Read your electric meter on the same day for three consecutive months (preferably the same day your utility company reads it) and record the numbers below:

1. _____ 2. _____ 3. _____

When you receive your electric bill, beginning with the second month, verify that you have used as much electricity as you have been charged for. (There may be minor discrepancies due to meter readings at different times. What you are looking for are major differences.) Are your readings and the utility company's readings consistent?

On each electric bill, verify that you are being billed at the correct rate, that the service charge is correct, and that the number of kilowatt-hours you have been billed for is appropriate. If you discover significant discrepancies, call your utility company and ask for an explanation.

When you've been away from your home or apartment for a week or more, monitor your bills. If there isn't a corresponding drop in your bill, find out why. There may be errors in the metering or billing process.

Be sure the utility meter reader can get to your meter. (If not, an estimate may be made that results in a much higher bill than you deserve.)

Use Your Utility Company's Services

Does your electric utility offer lower "off-peak" rates? _____

If so, is it feasible for you to take advantage of them? _____

Does your electric utility give rebates for the installation of electric heating or the purchase of energy-saving appliances such as water heaters, refrigerators, or air conditioners? (These rebates can add up to several hundred dollars.) If so, would it be to your advantage to make such a purchase? _____

Which of the following does your electric utility provide?

▲ A free energy audit. (If so, sign up!)
▲ Charts that show how much money small and large electric appliances cost to operate so you can better evaluate your usage.
▲ Other _____
▲ Other _____

INSULATE YOURSELF AGAINST HIGH HEATING AND COOLING BILLS

No matter where you live, three factors affect the heat flow within your home: conduction, infiltration, and radiation.

Conduction takes place when heat is transferred through the walls, ceilings, doors, windows, and floors of your home. When its interior is colder than the outside air, warm air is conducted into your home and heats the inside air. During the winter months, the heat in your home is conducted to the cooler outside air. If you are a homeowner, you can reduce conduction through proper levels of insulation. See pages 107–9 of *Living Smart, Spending Less*.

Infiltration allows outside air to penetrate your home through holes and cracks around doors and windows or when someone enters or leaves your home. A strong wind on a cold day clearly indicates where infiltration occurs. The greater the temperature difference between the inside of your home and the outside air, the more infiltration there will be.

Radiation from the sun affects the flow of heat into your home. During the summer, solar energy enters your home through windows, causing heat to build up unless you take steps to thwart it. During the winter, that solar energy can reduce your heating bills if you are able to capture it.

Ways to Reduce Infiltration

Air that leaks into your home makes a difference in your heating and cooling costs. To find out where cold or warm air is entering your home, carefully inspect for leaks where walls join the foundation and at the corners of siding where different building materials meet (such as brick and wood), and around doors, windows, water faucets, vents, and window air conditioning units. Another way to locate air leaks is to wear shorts and a T-shirt when it is cold outside and a strong wind is blowing!

Seal Up Those Leaks!

Once you discover the air leaks, you need to seal them. Using the chart below, inspect the following areas of your home, condo, or apartment and schedule a time to remedy any problems.

Location	Problem	Solution	Do When?
Interior ceiling or walls	Holes that allow inside air to enter the attic	Patch/repair the hole(s).	
Interior walls bordering the outside air	Electrical outlets that let in air	Turn off power to electrical circuit. Add a foam gasket behind the cover plate of each outlet and switch.	
Exterior of house	Deep and/or wide cracks that caulk won't fill	Use rope caulk around windows, an expanding foam sealant if larger holes and cracks aren't exposed to sunlight and moisture, etc.	
Doors and windows	Heat (or cooling) loss around doors and windows that open and close	Install weather stripping (choose one(s) designed for your specific need) or replace inefficient doors and windows.	
Doors, windows, vents, and outside faucets	Gaps around doors, windows, faucets, window air conditioner, or vents	Seal with caulk (ask which type is best for your specific need).	

Exterior of house or apartment	Unused dryer or exhaust vent that carries heated/cooled air outside	Cover or seal up each unused vent (but be careful not to seal necessary vents).	

KEEP COOL FOR LESS

People love warm, toasty homes. In the dead of winter, when ice storms pelt the South, a foot of snow lands on New England porches, or wind chills sweep across the Great Plains, we spend much time and money to keep the heat in our homes. But in the summer, when the thermometer climbs into the nineties and humidity soars, we try our best to keep the heat out. In this strange love/hate relationship, we even buy air conditioning systems to avoid the heat. Let's look at how you can spend less and still beat the heat!

How much you spend to keep your home cool depends on where you live (temperature, nearby vegetation, humidity level, type of winds), type and size of your home, the insulation in your home, local utility rates, your use of heat-producing appliances, and so on.

As you evaluate the following tips, consider which ones you can do easily. Note which ones you should do sooner than later, and try to work them in within the next few months. Finally, note ideas you might like to try if you have more time and money.

EVALUATE YOUR AIR CONDITIONING NEEDS

If you live in a temperate region where warm temperatures and humidity threaten only several weeks a year, do you need air conditioning? Consider using window fans.

If your home is relatively small and you spend more of your time in only a few rooms during the summer or if you are a renter, perhaps one or two high-efficency room air conditioning units, strategically placed, will do the job.

Perhaps a central air conditioning system will be the best. To determine whether central air is appropriate, consider the intensity and duration of the hot weather, your home's size, and your personal requirements.

Is a central air conditioning system a necessity for you? Why or why not? _____

_____

_____

SHOP FOR THE RIGHT AIR CONDITIONING UNIT

It's important to buy the right-sized unit for your home—not one that's too small or too large. The proper size and type of air conditioning unit is determined by:

✓ Square footage of the area to be cooled: _____

✓ Number of stories in your home: _____

✓ The size and placement of trees and shrubbery on the southern and
western sides: _____

✓ How hot and humid the climate is in your area: _____

✓ How often you use heat-producing appliances: _____

✓ The conservation measures you have taken or plan to take: _____

_____

Before you buy, comparison shop for the best price on the air conditioner that's right for you.

✓ If you must have a central air conditioning unit, consider one that has a high
Seasonal Energy Efficiency Ratio (SEER), which can dramatically reduce your
cooling costs. The federal government requires a minimum SEER of 10.0;
depending on your location, this may be adequate. Compare the initial cost of
the unit, expected savings compared to your present cooling system, your cash
flow, the length of time you plan to remain in your home, and how great your
need for cooling really is. If your cooling needs are more moderate, you probably
don't need a unit with as high an efficiency ratio and may be able to consider
less-expensive cooling options.

✓ Read independent analyses of various air conditioners.

✓ Evaluate warranties, serviceability, and dependability.

✓ Look for energy-saving features such as variable-speed fans that remove more
humidity from the air or switches that allow you to run the fan instead of the
whole unit.

✓ Finally, buy later in the summer when stores are more willing to lower
prices on cooling equipment.

GET MORE FOR YOUR AIR CONDITIONING BUCK

In addition to saving money on your initial purchase, you can save on your cooling
costs for the life of your air conditioner. Check off the money-saving cooling tips that you
regularly use:

❑ Operate the air conditioning unit(s) when electric rates may be lower.

❑ Don't block window air conditioning unit(s) with window coverings that keep
air from circulating.

❑ Tightly close exterior doors and windows when you run the air conditioner(s).

❑ Turn off window air conditioner(s) when you leave home for more than two
hours.

❑ Try to do your cooking early in the morning or later in the evening, when it's cooler outside.

❑ Maintain your unit's efficiency by doing maintenance you can safely do yourself (perhaps replacing the filter(s) regularly) and having a technician regularly perform other maintenance as recommended by the manufacturer.

❑ Raise the thermostat five degrees, and keep it away from direct sunlight and other heat sources.

Use Fans and Vents to Cool Your Home

One or more fans, used correctly, can also do a fine job of cooling a room or your whole house—at a fraction of what air conditioning costs. Investigate each of the following alternatives that interest you.

Cooling alternative:	Installation cost:	Annual operating cost:	Savings over air conditioning for installation and one year of operation:
A whole-house fan that draws warm air into the attic, vents it outside, and draws cooler air in through open windows	$	$	$
Variable-speed, reversible window fans (Be sure that children won't be able to stick their fingers near the fan blades.)	$	$	$
A variable-speed ceiling fan that circulates cooler air that settles near the floor	$	$	$
Portable fans that can be moved from room to room as needed	$	$	$
Operable skylights that vent heated air and allow cooler air from lower vents or windows to enter the house	$	$	$

Of course, fans are more than a low-cost alternative to air conditioning. They can also be used to supplement your air conditioning system and reduce air conditioning expenses.

Heat trapped in your attic can make it much more expensive to cool your home. How much would it cost to add extra vents, turbine fans, or thermostatically controlled exhaust fans in your attic? _____

Excess humidity makes the air feel warmer than it really is. Do you use a kitchen exhaust fan to remove cooking heat during the summer? _____

Do you use bathroom exhaust fans to remove moisture buildup after a bath or shower? _____

Use Shade to Your Advantage

Shade can dramatically reduce the amount of heat that enters through your home's windows, wall, and roof—up to 40 percent of your air conditioning energy. For more information on ways to keep cool, please refer to pages 117–20 in *Living Smart, Spending Less.*

KEEP WARM FOR LESS

For those who don't have the luxury of living in a well-insulated home, heating expenses can account for more than half of their annual energy costs. However, it is often possible to substantially reduce heating costs with moderate effort and a little expense. As you read the following tips, carefully consider which ones you can and should do given your housing situation. Each tip can make a difference!

Keep Your Furnace in Tip-Top Shape

Unless your house is completely heated by solar equipment, wood, or electricity, you probably depend on some kind of furnace or boiler to provide primary heat. To get the most heat at the lowest cost, follow these tips:

❏ Keep up on routine maintenance. Furnaces should be inspected and adjusted (usually annually) so they will run efficiently.
❏ When was the last time your furnace was serviced? _____
(If it's time for servicing, schedule a date today!)
❏ For the greatest savings, schedule maintenance during the summer when service rates are cheaper.
❏ You can save money by learning the maintenance you can do—and what a heating technician must do. Write down the maintenance tasks you can do and how often they must be done.

    1. _____

2. _____

3. _____

❏ Detect heating problems early. Prompt attention could save you quite a bit of money.

Make the Most of the Heat You Have

Once you've paid for heat, there's no point in losing its effectiveness! From which of the following tips could you benefit?

Heat Saver	Already Do	Will Try
Direct heated air where you want it to go by using air deflectors on floor registers.		
Move furniture and draperies away from heating ducts, baseboards, and radiators so that heated air can circulate freely.		
Tape heavy-duty aluminum foil to insulation board, and slip it between the wall and the radiator or baseboard convector. (But don't restrict proper air circulation between the wall and radiator.)		
Use exhaust vents sparingly. They carry out lots of heated air.		
Plant evergreens and/or shrubs on the northern and northwestern sides of your home to break harsh winter winds. (Don't plant them so close to the house that they trap moisture near the walls.)		
Maintain appropriate humidity levels in your home during the winter months. Humidity makes the air seem warmer.		
Wear warm clothing inside. A heavy, long-sleeved sweater adds about four degrees of warmth.[9]		
Minimize heat loss through windows and doors. (See section on insulation/infiltration for details.)		

You can also supplement your furnace heat by making the most of the sun's warmth. Which of the following suggestions apply to your situation?

✓ Remove screens on the southern side of your home so you'll receive the maximum amount of solar gain.

✓ Wash south-facing windows more frequently during the winter.

✓ Install heat-absorbing flooring in areas that receive lots of sunlight. (Dark-colored tile or brick laid on concrete will absorb solar heat during the day and release it at night.)

✓ Open curtains, windows, or blinds on windows that receive direct sunlight.

What other ways can you take advantage of the sun's warmth during winter months?

_____

_____

Ways to Keep Warm for Less Money

It seems that we can always use new ideas for saving money while keeping warm. One of the best ways is to lower thermostats.

DID YOU KNOW . . . that reducing the temperature by five degrees overnight can save you up to 10 percent on fuel costs? And every degree over seventy degrees typically adds 3 percent to your heating bill.[10]

Check the thermostat tricks you regularly use, then add your own to the list:

❑ When you leave home for several days or longer, turn thermostats down but not so low that pipes freeze during your absence.

❑ Install a programmable thermostat that automatically lowers the temperature in your home when no one is there or while you sleep.

❑ If someone opens a bedroom window at night during the heating season, close the door to his or her room. If there's a thermostat in the room, turn it down.

❑ Other _____

❑ Other _____

If you find that lowering thermostats leaves you a bit chilly at times, you can warm up by:

❑ Using an electric blanket according to proper instructions.

❑ Using a small, laboratory-tested heater when you need a little extra heat in a specific area or room. (But do not use a portable electric heater in the bathroom or other areas that are often wet.)

❑ Other _____

Now that you have finished this portion of the workbook, you may begin to see significant savings on your home energy costs. Keep track of your savings—it's good encouragement to continue living smart and spending less!

1. Doris B. Gill, *My Houseful of Hints: How to Solve Problems at Home and Away* (Walnut Creek, Calif.: Crab Cove, 1989), 78.
2. George B. Roscoe, *Today's Energy Saver's Guide for Homeowners* (Washington, DC: Acropolis, 1978), 8.
3. *Tips for Energy Savers* (Washington, DC: U.S. Dept. of Energy, n.d.), 13.
4. Ibid.
5. Ibid.
6. Ralph J. Herbert, *Cut Your Electric Bills in Half* (Emmaus, Pa.: Rodale, 1986), 86.
7. Robert Derven and Carol Nichols, *How to Cut Your Energy Bills*, 2d ed. (Farmington, Mich.: Structures, 1980), 102.
8. *Tips for Energy Savers*, 6.
9. Carol Rees, *Household Hints for Upstairs, Downstairs, and All Around the House* (New York: Henry Holt, 1982), 22.
10. Roscoe, *Today's Energy Saver's Guide for Homeowners*, 50.

6
Hail! Wind! Fire! And Other Household Hazards

Every day, in cities and towns worldwide, good people face tough challenges. Apartments and houses catch on fire, rousing people from their beds and destroying their belongings. Tornadoes scatter a lifetime's possessions. Hailstorms pound outbuildings, boats, and trailers. Sewers back up and water pipes break. Someone is injured in a home or on a property. Can these things happen to you or me? Sadly, they can. Fortunately, a good homeowner's or renter's insurance policy and a good company that stands behind it will make a big difference when you face situations such as these.

The right homeowner's or renter's insurance policy can save you money by protecting your home and its contents, and providing liability coverage while other people are on your property. If you are a homeowner, the policy typically will pay additional living expenses you may incur if your home is severely damaged. For most people, homeowner's insurance is mandatory because they don't actually own their homes and their mortgage companies require adequate insurance coverage to protect their investment. Buying renter's insurance is also important, so that renters' possessions are covered against loss by wind, fire, flood, theft, and other perils. We will focus primarily on how to buy homeowner's insurance in order to save hundreds of dollars or more.

YOUR INSURANCE CHECKLIST

The following steps will help ensure that you have the best homeowner's/renter's policy for your current needs. If you already have a homeowner's or renter's insurance policy, review it carefully, then complete the following questions to determine your current needs. If you are presently uninsured, use this insurance checklist as a guideline to help you understand the types of coverage available and determine the type of coverage you need.

Type of coverage you have

Check the type of coverage you now have (or would consider):

- ☐ The basic HO-1 policy covering your house and its contents against eleven basic perils
- ☐ A broader HO-3 policy that covers many more kinds of losses than the basic policy, including the weight of ice
- ☐ An HO-5 policy that covers the house and its contents for all perils, except those your policy specifically excludes
- ☐ A tenant's policy (HO-4) that covers a number of risks to personal property and provides limited liability coverage, not including liability resulting from the use of an automobile
- ☐ An HO-8 policy for an older home
- ☐ An HO-6 policy for a condominium

What is your current deductible amount? _____

If you can pay $500 or $1,000 out of pocket instead of $250 or $100 in the event of a claimable loss, consider selecting the higher deductible if the difference in premium makes the change cost effective. What is the highest deductible you would consider?

_____

Does your policy automatically adjust for inflation or replacement building costs?

_____

If you do not have this type of coverage, how much would you be willing to pay for it? _____

Policy exclusions and limitations

When evaluating a current or prospective policy, know its limitations. If, for instance, you live in a flood-prone region, are you covered for flood damage? What about snow and ice damage? Sewer backups? Plumbing leaks? Earthquakes? Smoke damage? What if your freezer quits working and your food spoils?

List the specific losses (such as those described above) for which you are insured:

_____

_____

_____

_____

List the losses for which you are *not* insured that you should consider:

_____

_____

_____

_____

Which of the following personal property coverages do you have?

☐ Standard coverage, which will repair a damaged item or pay for the cost of replacing the damaged item minus depreciation.

☐ Replacement-cost coverage, which will pay the full cost of replacing or repairing damaged property with like kind and quality at current prices. In order to qualify for this coverage, you must maintain coverage for at least 80 percent of your home's replacement value. (Note: In many instances, replacement-cost coverage may not cost much more than less comprehensive kinds of coverage.)

☐ Scheduled coverage, which insures items of special value at an additional premium. Each item must be appraised and listed separately.

What is the coverage limit on your personal effects? _____

Does your policy have limits on coverage for certain categories of valuable personal property? (Rare coins, antiques, silver, guns, expensive jewelry, furs, and the like may be subject to a maximum coverage of as little as a few hundred dollars unless you "schedule" these items separately and pay an additional premium to have them covered.) What are the limits of your policy on each category?

1. _____

2. _____

3. _____

4. _____

5. _____

In light of the limitations of your policy, list each item (and its value) that you should "schedule" separately. (If you need more room, use a separate sheet of paper.)

_____

_____

_____

_____

Appropriate coverage for your current needs

There is no such thing as a one-fits-all insurance policy. Your policy should cover the types of losses most appropriate to your living situation. You need to discuss your unique requirements with your agent. The following checklist of unique situations may help you identify insurance needs that you don't want to overlook.

○ You've made significant improvements to your home that have increased its value. (Make sure your home is not underinsured.)

○ You have a detached building(s) (storage shed, garage, barn).

○ A renter lives with you.

○ You have an indoor or outdoor pool.

○ You operate a business out of your home. (Do you need special coverage for equipment, inventory, or liability?)

○ You have a computer or other expensive equipment in an office in your home even though you are generally employed elsewhere.

○ You own animals other than typical household pets. (Will your liability coverage include any damage or injury they might do to others? What exclusions or limitations apply to this coverage?)

○ You haven't paid off your home. (What type and level of coverage does the mortgage company require you to carry?)

○ You have recently acquired more personal property, so the amount of coverage you presently have may be insufficient.

Existing policy and costs

How much does your existing policy cost you a year? $_____

Is your present level of insurance adequate?_____ (If your home is not insured for all of its replacement value—which may be different from the market or resale value—the insurance company will not pay for losses beyond the policy limit. And if the home is not insured for at least 80 percent of replacement cost, the company will pay only a portion of the full amount on a claim, even if the claim is for less than the limit of your policy.)

If not, what should your new policy limits be? _____

Which coverage(s) should you add to your present policy? What will each additional or scheduled coverage cost?

Additional Coverage	Additional Premium

COMPARE COMPANIES, POLICIES, AND PRICES

You may be thinking, *OK, I've done a thorough review of my policy and have been with the same company for years. Why do I have to take time to compare companies, policies, and prices?* And if you're buying homeowner's insurance for the first time, you may be thinking, *I'll get insurance with the same company that insures my car. Why should I call around to get price quotes and compare prices?*

Those are good questions, and the answers are the same. Companies change. Policies change. Prices change. Sometimes those changes are in your favor; other times, they are not. The only way to keep track of whether your policy is the best one you can afford is to compare it with others in the marketplace.

The following suggestions could save you hundreds of dollars a year and lead you to even better coverage than you have now. See which ones fit your situation and decide to apply them soon.

Select companies

At the library, research the reputation and financial health of several insurance companies. Use the publications of A. M. Best Company, Moody's Investors Service, Inc., and/or Standard & Poor's Corporation for your research.

What is the rating of your present company? (Note: The type of ratings may be different in each publication; what's important is for the company to be in one of the highest-rated categories.)

A. M. Best Company rating: _____

Moody's Investors Service, Inc. rating: _____

Standard & Poor's Corporation rating: _____

Which insurance companies have your friends and/or family members been pleased with, particularly when it comes to service and claims adjustment?

1. _____

2. _____

3. _____

4. _____

Check the ratings of each of these companies and choose the ones from which you will solicit quotes.

1. _____

2. _____

3. _____

Compare companies

Using the information you gained when you reviewed your existing policy, determine the personal property coverage that fits your situation, including the deductible you'd like to have. Then contact the companies you researched—as well as the company you may currently be using—and compare policies and price quotations.

Type of Coverage	Amount of Coverage	Deductible Amount	Co. #1	Co. #2	Co. #3
Dwelling					
Personal Property					
Liability					
Medical Payments					
Loss of Use					
Additional Coverage					
Scheduled Coverage					
Discounts					
TOTAL PREMIUM					

As you talk with each agent on the telephone, be sure to ask for the same coverage requirements so that the quotations you receive will be accurate and can be accurately compared. (If an outbuilding needs to be insured, for example, make sure it is included in each quote.) Ask the agent to send you a sample policy and written quote so you can evaluate it for yourself and call back with any questions. (There is greater chance of mis-communication and inaccuracy through telephone quotations than through written ones!)

Also discuss with each agent each of the following points.

▲ How does the deductible amount you can easily afford compare in premium cost to the deductible amount one level higher and one level lower?

▲ How much more is a policy that automatically adjusts for inflation or replacement building costs?

▲ What is the price of replacement-cost coverage compared to standard coverage?

▲ What are the policy's limitations and exclusions?

▲ Discount opportunities. You may be eligible for a discount if one or more of the following applies to you:

    ❐ You are retired and/or a senior citizen.

    ❐ You work at home.

    ❐ You abstain from smoking and/or drinking alcohol.

    ❐ Excellent fire protection is available in your area.

    ❐ You have marked your valuables with identification numbers.

    ❐ You seem to be "low risk" because of few claims and/or the neighborhood in which you live.

    ❐ You plan to insure your car(s) with the same company that insures your home or apartment.

    ❐ You have installed smoke detectors, alarms, fire extinguishers, and/or sprinklers in your home.

    ❐ You have installed deadbolt locks and/or burglar alarms.

When you have completed your research, compare all the new policy information you have discovered and the costs of the coverage you need, and make your choice. When you do, ask your agent about premium payment options. Some companies offer quarterly or monthly payments, rather than annual payments, at no additional charge to you. Other companies charge interest or a service fee for this convenience.

A FINAL NOTE: KNOW WHAT YOU OWN

It's always wise to inventory your goods so you know what you own in the event you suffer a loss. This is true no matter which insurance company and policy you select.

Although we each like to think we know each item in our home, our memories can fade—after a traumatic, near-total loss—when we need to reconstruct a list of everything missing. From the attic to the basement, from original cost to serial numbers, the only way most of us can remember our possessions is to inventory them. Yes, this is a lot of work, but if you ever need the list, you'll be glad you have it. Here, step by step, is a plan to list your belongings. Check off each one as you do it. (Your insurance company may provide an inventory booklet in which you can list each item, room by room.)

❏ Write descriptions of your goods, including serial and model numbers, prices paid, and where and when you purchased them.

❏ Photograph or videotape antiques, special collections, furniture, kitchen cabinets, tools in the garage, and pictures on the wall.

❏ Photograph or videotape open drawers, open cabinets, open closets, shelves, and so on.

❏ Photograph, videotape, or fully describe any custom features in your home that would add to its replacement cost. These might include high-performance windows, extensive wood paneling or custom woodwork, a custom-designed kitchen, built-in furniture, and/or heating/cooling filtration equipment required for special medical needs.

❏ Photograph or videotape any outbuildings, the outside of your home, valuable trees on your property, and recreational equipment such as boats and camping trailers.

❏ Locate appraisals and receipts for expensive items.

Store your inventory in a safe place! Put the inventory of your goods—including appraisals, receipts, and photographs or videotapes—into a lockbox or other safe location *away from where you live*. If you store them at home and your house or apartment is badly damaged or destroyed, the information you'll need to begin the insurance process could be damaged or destroyed.

7
Buying and Caring for Clothing

We'd all agree that clothing is an unavoidable need in human life. We need it to protect us from weather and to make us feel comfortable in the presence of others. But clothing has come to mean much more than personal protection. We use it as a way of revealing (or masking) our identity, as a way of communicating our financial or social status, and as a way of influencing the opinions others have of us.

With such powerful motivators influencing our clothing choices, it's no wonder that the amount of money we spend on clothing can get out of hand. Yet there are ways to reduce what we spend on clothing—and to do so without lessening the quality of our wardrobe.

Few of us automatically know how to stretch clothing dollars. Most of us have to learn how to make wise choices on a consistent basis. Here's how to evaluate your shopping style, learn how to buy only what you need, and learn how to buy for the long term.

EVALUATE YOUR SHOPPING STYLE

In order to save money on clothing, it's important to take an honest look at what motivates you to buy clothing the way you do. Carefully answer the following questions. No one else needs to know your answers, so be honest!

Describe your shopping "style." Where do you prefer to shop: store to store in a mall, at secondhand stores, in exclusive boutiques, from catalogs, or some other approach? Do you buy only what you need, or whatever strikes your fancy?

I _____

_____

_____

_____.

When you shop, what is most important to you?

❑ Selection ❑ Price ❑ Proximity to home/work ❑ Sales staff
❑ Quality ❑ Name Brands ❑ Other _____

List the clothing stores in which you generally shop. Write down why you shop in each.

1. _____

2. _____

3. _____

4. _____

In what ways do you think your present shopping style helps you save money? Costs you money? _____

_____

_____

In what way(s) might your attitudes toward shopping limit your choices? (Are there places you would never shop, for example?) _____

_____

In what way(s) does the amount of time you have available to shop influence your shopping? _____

_____

To what degree does the amount of money you have available to spend on clothing dictate where you shop? _____

_____

In what way(s) does the image you have to maintain in your workplace (or socially) influence your clothing decisions? (Consider the impact of this image on your choices of personal as well as professional clothing.) _____

How much does it cost you to maintain this image? How might you achieve the same result for less money? _____

_____

_____

As a rule, are you patient enough to wait until items go on sale instead of buying on impulse? What impact does this answer have on your buying decisions?_____

_____

Are you willing to comparison shop for your clothing ? Why or why not?

_____

_____

Are you willing to explore new possibilities to find the clothes you want or need at lower prices? Why or why not? _____

_____

How might you change your present shopping habits in order to save money?

_____

_____

Buy Only What You Need

Avoid impulse buying. Most people have items in their closets or in boxes that were purchased on impulse. Often these items are rarely, if ever, worn. The following process will help you evaluate your buying history and show you how to limit your clothing purchases to the items you really need.

- ❑ Carefully look through your closet(s). Remove items that do not fit well, are worn-out, or will never suit your present or future needs. (Be tough here! Otherwise this exercise won't do you any good.)
- ❑ Now, test yourself! Separate the clothing you no longer want or need into two piles: one for the items you planned to purchase, and one for the items you bought on impulse. Which pile is larger? What does this tell you about your impulse buying history? _____

_____

❏ Determine which of the items you no longer need can be:
1. Given to friends.
2. Given to a church or organization that distributes clothing to needy people.
3. Sold on consignment at a resale store.
4. Thrown away.

❏ Give, sell, or toss those items, and then take a hard look at what is left in your closet. List the particular items you need to buy. Keep in mind the following:

(1) You might be able to build a wardrobe using the garments you already have; new accessories might make an old standby seem new again.

(2) You may be able to wear certain clothing items for more than one season of the year (such as a medium-weight sweater or a certain type of dress or suitcoat).

(3) Each new item should have a purpose (casual use, specific sporting activity, dressy occasion, everyday professional use, and so on) and have needed durability.

The chart below will help you plan your necessary clothing purchases. First, describe specifically the item(s) you need to purchase in each category. Then indicate the time frame in which you need to purchase the items. (This chart will help you budget for expensive clothing purchases such as coats and suits. If you desire, indicate approximate price in the description.) We have included several examples to show you how to use the chart to your advantage.

Descriptions of items you need	Buy now	Buy within 6 months	Buy within 1 year
Shoes: *black pumps for office — medium heel*	X		
Running shoes		X	
Pants/Slacks: *tan casual slacks — summer weight*		X	
Skirts: *black wool to go with herringbone blazer*			X
Dresses:			
Shirts/Blouses:			
Sweaters:			

Coats/Jackets:			
Sport Jackets/Blazers:			
Suits:			
Socks:			
Underwear:			
Accessories:			
Other:			

BUY FOR THE LONG TERM

The maxim for the fashion scene is "new is better; toss out last season's look in favor of this season's hottest fashion." Following that advice can destroy a budget, and it ignores the benefits of having a classic style that you can wear again and again. A key to saving money is to see through the fashion game and to buy basic, well-made items that will stand the test of time—and to buy those items at a reasonable price. The tips and questions below will help you discover the secrets of savvy shopping.

☞ Be Only as Fashion Conscious as You Can Afford to Be.

Fashions come and go, but basic, classic styles can be worn for years. Choose clothing that won't look outdated six months after you buy it.

Your answers to the following questions can help you distinguish between the always "in" classic look and the trendy look. What characteristics of today's trendy styles may be passé next season? _____

_____

_____

In contrast, what are the characteristics of styles that "will stand the test of time" and be worn for years? _____

_____

_____

What are the advantages and disadvantages of dressing in the latest "in" clothing?

_____

_____

☞ Shop for Multi-Season Clothing.

If you buy clothing that can be worn for two to three seasons of the year rather than just one, you have fewer items to pack up, store, and unpack again when the weather changes. For example, instead of buying a heavy winter coat and a lighter-weight coat for fall (and perhaps a lighter-weight coat in a different color for spring), consider buying one medium-weight coat that will be comfortable during fall and spring and then add a liner or wear a sweater to obtain greater warmth during the winter months.

Describe the types of clothing you can wear for several seasons of the year in your locale: _____

_____

_____

☞ Evaluate Material and Workmanship Before You Buy.

Unfortunately, much clothing today is not made well and won't last long even under normal use. So it's important to learn some basic points of comparison. Can you, for example, recognize a strong seam or a straight hem when you see one? Do you know how well certain types of fabric will wear? Do you know which fabrics tend to be cooler or warmer? Can you tell whether or not a lapel will keep its shape over time? What can a quick glance at a seam tell you about the quality of a garment?

If you're not sure of the answers to these questions, find them. A trip to your local library or a conversation with a knowledgeable salesperson at a quality clothing establishment can help you learn. And if you think about it, your own experience can be a great teacher.

Consider, for instance, the clothing that hasn't held up well for you. In what ways did the garments fail to perform? _____

_____

What would you look for in order to recognize these potential problems in future items you purchase? _____

_____

☞ Pay Attention to the Comfort Factor.

Clothing that lasts should be comfortable too. Whenever possible, try on an article of clothing before you buy it. It should not itch, pinch, or restrict. Whether you buy from a retail store or a catalog, make sure you can return any items that don't fit well for a full refund or at least a credit toward another purchase. (The exception to this would be a used clothing store where returns may not be possible but the savings more than make up for the risk.)

List the comfort factors that are particularly important to you so you know what to look for in future purchases. (Loose necks, sleeves that aren't too long or too short? Plenty of shoulder room? Comfortable waistbands?)

_____

_____

☞ Buy for Special Occasions.

Buying for a special occasion may be fun, but it can be expensive too! Yet it's possible to purchase special occasion clothing you can wear again and again.

Describe the kinds of special occasions you most frequently attend: _____

_____

_____

Now describe the clothing and accessories that will be dressy enough for the most formal occasions but not too dressy for less-formal occasions. Be sure to consider the following: Short or long? Dress, pants, skirt, or suit? Which accessories can "dress up" or "dress down" a basic outfit? What color options do you have, or should you stick with classic black? _____

_____

_____

When you need a clothing item that you are likely to wear only once, you may be able to purchase a less-expensive garment that will look great but may not stand up to long-term use. Another option is to find an inexpensive, but high-quality item in a consignment shop. If the latter option appeals to you, list some quality consignment shops near your home or office and plan to visit them when the need arises: _____

_____

_____

☞ Concentrate on a Basic Color Group.

Stephen's father once told him, "I've chosen to go with blues and grays instead of using browns too. That way, I can mix and match." His good advice has enabled Stephen to save lots of money through the years.

When you focus on compatible color groups, it's easy to adapt to changing styles. For example, a classic shirt or blouse that goes with navy slacks or a skirt can be used for a number of years, no matter how much the slack or skirt styles change. It also becomes easy to create variety in your wardrobe, especially when you pick up complementary accessories such as ties, belts, or scarves.

Which colors look best on you? If you're not sure which colors are best for you, have a good color analysis done or ask a clothes-conscious friend or spouse to tell you which colors work. That friend can also accompany you when you shop and point out clothing that looks good and fits well on you.

☞ Combine Outfits.

If a suitcoat no longer fits or has become dated, you may still be able to wear the suit pants or skirt with a different suitcoat. Take time to survey possible clothing combinations.

CARE FOR WHAT YOU HAVE

To get the most from your clothing dollars, learn the best ways to care for your clothing so you can keep new purchases to a minimum.

☞ Follow Cleaning Instructions.

Whether it's made of a delicate fabric, a hardy cotton, or a permanent press blend, all clothing deserves special care during washings. A new shirt can fade or lose its crispness before its time if faced with constant hot washes and hot dryings. Some fabric will shrink under certain conditions. By failing to follow instructions, you could be out the money you paid for the item, plus the time and money it takes to replace it.

☞ Repair or Alter Worn Clothing.

Clothing often can get a breath of life with help from a needle and thread. Go to your closet and gather together all of your clothing that needs repair or alteration—especially those items you haven't worn in ages simply because they are missing a button or have a few stitches out in the hem. Schedule a time, perhaps while you watch a movie at home, to tackle the mending pile.

☞ Dress Down for Dirty Tasks.

It is wise to set aside an outfit or two that you wear only when doing dirty tasks. It beats staining or otherwise damaging your good clothes.

What older clothing could you set aside for such tasks? _____

_____

☞ Take the Clothing Care Quiz.

Clothing that is cared for will last longer and look nicer than neglected clothing. Test yourself on how many of the following clothing care tips you regularly follow. Do you:

❏ Repair tears promptly so they don't get worse?
❏ Repair loose buttons before they fall off?
❏ Fix unraveling hems promptly? (Note: "fixing" hems with tape doesn't count!)
❏ Hang up or fold your clothing as soon as you take it off rather than piling it on a chair?
❏ Avoid hanging clothing where the sun might fade it?
❏ Try to keep clothing in your closet from becoming dusty?
❏ Hang clothing on wooden or plastic hangers instead of wire hangers?
❏ Use "suit hangers" contoured for coats, jackets, and suits?
❏ Avoid leaving sharp or staining objects (like nails and pens) in your pockets?
❏ Watch what you sit on or lean against to avoid tar, gum, etc.?
❏ Use the coolest temperature setting possible when drying clothes?
❏ Treat stains promptly, before they "set"?
❏ Wash delicate clothing by hand instead of by machine? Or place delicate items into a mesh bag and select the "gentle" cycle?
❏ Carry a water-resistant jacket or umbrella so you can protect good clothes from rain?
❏ Wear old clothing to do work around the house?

Total Check Marks:____

How many items did you check? If you scored ten or more, congratulations! You have mastered many of the tasks necessary in stretching a wardrobe.

SHOPPING SKILLS CHECKLIST

Answer each of these questions and explain why you do what you do.

101

❑ Am I willing to wait until an item I want or need goes on sale? _____

_____

❑ Do I compare prices on basic items, such as jeans, sweats, socks, T-shirts, shoes, and underwear? _____

_____

❑ Do I shop at stores that have good refund/return policies? _____

_____

❑ Do I keep a receipt until after I have worn and washed an item, so I can return it if I need to? _____

❑ Am I willing to return an item that doesn't satisfy me and ask for a refund/credit? _____

❑ Do I shop seasonally, stocking up on summer items in the fall and on winter items in the spring? _____

WHERE TO FIND THOSE SPECIAL DEALS

It's possible to find great deals and save money on clothing just about anywhere—even in stores that are normally high priced. The key is to keep your eyes open wherever you shop. In order to save the most on clothing, however, it's also important to learn about the discount stores in your area. These include, but are not limited to, the following.

Factory Outlets

These stores sell a variety of items—sometimes at up to 80 percent off. If you're serious about finding the best deals in this area, check your local library for books that list factory outlets by region. Also check phone books and talk with knowledgeable friends.

List any factory outlets in your area and the type of goods they sell:

1. _____

2. _____

3. _____

4. _____

Specialty Outlets

Generally specializing in one type of merchandise such as shoes, fabric, men's suits, kitchenware, and so on, specialty outlets buy surplus inventory from manufacturers or merchandise at manufacturers' "distress sales." Some outlets offer great savings on quality goods; other outlets offer inferior, "irregular," flawed, and/or damaged products. So be careful.

Which specialty outlets in your area are worth investigating?

1. _____
2. _____
3. _____
4. _____

Non-Member Discount Stores

Sometimes these stores sell low-end items for low prices. We have found good buys on children's clothing, swimsuits, underwear, socks, and some accessories. Some discount stores offer better prices on certain categories of clothing. (One may have the best prices on children's clothing; another may have the best prices on shoes.) As always, consider quality as well as price.

In which non-member discount stores in your area have you found the best deals? For which categories of clothing?

1. _____
2. _____
3. _____

Garage Sales and Flea Markets

If you have the time, garage sales and flea markets can be great places to find clothing "treasures." Sometimes you'll find exactly what you need. Other times, nothing turns up for weeks. We've purchased great items for literally pennies, but we've also seen clothing that is priced way too high or junk that shouldn't even be up for sale.

Just for fun, what is the best garage sale or flea market bargain you've found?

_____

Where and how often are the flea markets held in your area?

1. _____
2. _____

3. _____

The following tips will help you in your garage sale and flea market "treasure hunting." Feel free to add your own ideas.

- ❏ Use the local newspaper to locate garage sales/flea markets that may have items in which you are interested.
- ❏ Carry cash, including small bills, to increase your bargaining power. If a seller sees a larger bill, the price may suddenly go up.
- ❏ Know what the items you're interested in buying cost in retail stores so you don't pay too much.
- ❏ Know the specific requirements of the item(s) you're looking for (size, color, length, and so on).
- ❏ Don't be afraid to offer a low price. It doesn't always work, but a casual "Will you take $5 for this?" often brings great results!
- ❏ For the best selection, visit garage sales in exclusive neighborhoods as soon as they open.
- ❏ _____
- ❏ _____

Secondhand/Thrift Stores

These stores, which can be found almost anywhere, include consignment shops, charity thrift stores, and privately owned thrift stores. They generally offer used clothing but may offer brand-new clothing too. You can save lots of money if you shop in them regularly and know your merchandise.

Write down the names and locations of the secondhand/thrift stores listed in the telephone directory. Visit each one several times, and note which ones seem to carry the clothing you need. Also note which ones aren't worth visiting again!

Store/location	Merchandise notes	Visit 1	Visit 2	Visit 3

The following tips, when put into practice, can help you make the most of thrift/secondhand store shopping. Check the ones that appeal to you.

❑ When you're in the area, drop into stores that stock what you need.

❑ Shop when inclement weather reduces customer traffic.

❑ Stock up on everyday clothing items when you find them at affordable prices.

❑ Be patient—willing to wait until the right clothing comes along.

❑ Be willing to bargain when price is negotiable.

❑ Learn each store's clothing strengths and weaknesses. Perhaps at one store nothing you like ever turns up except skirts and jackets.

❑ Learn when special sales are held in each store.

❑ Know which clothes you need—and carry a tape measure.

❑ Try on clothing whenever possible before you buy it.

❑ Scan the racks quickly.

❑ Pay close attention to wear areas—knees, seats, cuffs, elbows, zippers, buttons—before you buy an item.

❑ Test all zippers and buttons to make sure they work or are worth fixing.

❑ Check for stains.

❑ Dress appropriately. If there's room to bargain, you'll lose if you look like a million dollars!

❑ Become familiar with which brands of clothing tend to fit you.

❑ Again, wear lighter-weight clothing whenever possible (shorts in the summer, for example) so you can try on clothing if the store doesn't provide dressing rooms.

Catalog Shopping

Depending on what you need, you can find good deals in direct-mail catalogs. This is particularly true if you are shopping for unusual or especially high-quality items that you might otherwise have to find in a specialty shop. Use mail-order companies that offer good products and terms, unbeatable guarantees, and reasonable prices.

Which catalogs, if any, have you found useful? _____

_____

What, for you, are the advantages and disadvantages of catalog shopping? Do these make catalog shopping a good value for you? _____

_____

If you're already a catalog shopper, read the following checklist and check off any areas in which you can "improve" in your shopping savvy.

❑ Am I sure about a catalog company's reputation before I order something from it? (If not, contact the Chamber of Commerce and/or Better Business Bureau and ask if there are any outstanding complaints about the company.)

❑ Am I leery of "contests" or "giveaways" that encourage impulse spending?

❑ Do I understand the terms of my purchase (including who is responsible for lost goods), delivery dates, the return policy, and the policy on substitutions if an item I order is out of stock?

❑ Do I ask the company for a refund if I haven't received the item(s) I ordered within thirty days? (In most instances, the company is required to provide one.)

❑ Do I keep a record of what I order—its price, description, when I placed the order, and how much I paid for it?

❑ Am I always careful to give my credit card number(s) only to reputable companies?

Tips for Buying Children's Clothing

If you buy clothing for children, you know the following is true: "Trees grow, weeds grow, and kids grow even faster than weeds." So buying clothing for children is an ongoing challenge.

Which of the following tips can you put into practice this week?

❑ Buy clothing on sale that your child(ren) will grow into.

❑ Choose basic, "undated" styles of clothing.

❑ Shop discount and thrift stores regularly.

❑ Take advantage of seasonal sales.

❑ Trade clothing with friends and family members.

❑ Avoid clothing with tight necks and sleeves that restrict children's movements.

❑ If you "love" a particular article of clothing, but you suspect your child won't like it, save your money and buy something else!

❑ Select clothing that can be altered as the child(ren) grows.

❑ When possible, have the child(ren) try on clothing before you buy it.

❑ Check all zippers, buttons, and wear areas for durability and ease of use.

❑ Try on coats and swimsuits when the child is wearing clothing similar to what he or she will wear under those garments.

Don't Forget Your Feet!

There's no way to get around our need for shoes. Although shoe prices continue to climb, you can save quite a bit on shoe purchases. Which of the following tips do you practice when you go shoe shopping? Those areas not receiving check marks may suggest new strategies that you can adopt to keep dollars in your pocket.

❏ I always try on shoes before buying them. The way a shoe fits depends a lot on style and workmanship, not just size.

❏ For the greatest long-term value, I look for practical, well-made shoes that will stand the test of time and that can be resoled and reheeled.

❏ I choose medium- or dark-colored shoes when I can. They don't show as much dirt as lighter colors do.

❏ I watch for shoe sales. And I keep my eyes open for seasonal closeouts. (This can really save you dollars. Stephen recently bought four pairs of top-quality athletic shoes for less than seven dollars a pair—marked down from $65 to $75 a pair!)

❏ If a pair of almost-new shoes in a thrift shop fits, I buy it. Then I spray each shoe with a fungicide before wearing it.

Great Clothing Bargains

For fun and encouragement, keep a record of your greatest clothing bargains, or chart your savings over a six-month or one-year period. You'll be surprised by how much you can save.

8
Saving Money on Food

The old adage "What goes up must come down" applies to many things: the snowball our daughter throws at us, the kite that soars higher and higher until a sudden change in wind direction or velocity sends it plummeting to the ground. But as we shop for food, we've noticed that once a food item goes up in price, it usually stays there . . . or goes higher.

But no matter what food prices are doing at any given time, there are ways to get the most from your food dollar. As in all shopping, advance planning is the key to spending less.

Some people make spending less money on food a time-consuming effort. They drive all over town to save a few cents. Others who are eager to reduce their food costs buy oats in fifty-pound bags and eat porridge every morning. Is there a happy balance? You bet! On the following pages, you'll have the opportunity to explore your food-buying habits and consider the money-saving changes you may wish to make.

IDENTIFY YOUR FOOD-BUYING HABITS

The following checklists will help you evaluate how you buy food. Check off whichever food-buying practices apply to you. At the end of each list, total the number of check marks (✓). Then learn what your score means.

How I shop:

- ❏ I tend to buy food when I'm hungry.
- ❏ I often buy items that are prominently featured in the grocery store, whether I need them or not.
- ❏ When I try a food sample in the grocery store, I feel compelled to buy it.
- ❏ I often grocery shop with a child or spouse who influences what I buy.
- ❏ I buy a lot of ready-to-eat and easy-to-prepare foods, such as snacks, deli foods, and microwavable meals, because I don't take time to cook more wholesome foods that may take longer to prepare.
- ❏ I rarely go into a grocery store with a list of what I need.
- ❏ When I shop, I just buy whatever looks good to me that day.
- ❏ I hate spending time in a grocery store, so I just pick up what I need as quickly as possible—without looking at competing brands or comparing prices.

Total:_____ If you checked any of these, you may be spending many dollars extra each week at the grocery store.

My money-saving efforts:

- ❏ I try generic products and house brands that may be cheaper than name brands.
- ❏ I use coupons to buy foods I'd normally buy anyway.
- ❏ I shop anywhere that I find wholesome, nutritious foods at good prices—the supermarket, health food store, farmer's market.
- ❏ I am willing to cut up a whole chicken or buy sale meat in bulk and repackage it to freeze and use later.
- ❏ Instead of buying pre-sliced meat, I buy a larger portion and ask the butcher to slice it for me.
- ❏ I try to buy the food items that I regularly eat when they're on sale.
- ❏ I buy lower-priced foods, even if they will take longer to prepare than some other options.
- ❏ When it's appropriate, I buy some foods in quantity.

Total: _____ If you scored four or more, you're saving many dollars each week at the grocery store. Try to raise your score—and savings—by adopting more of the above strategies.

Planning:

1. ❏ I have never bothered to compare the prices of items I usually buy between two or more stores.

2. ❏ I don't know how much I spend on food each month.
3. ❏ I usually shop on my way home from work. My planning starts when I leave the office and includes dinner and the next morning's breakfast.
4. ❏ I often compare grocery store sales flyers and plan my menus according to what's on sale that week.
5. ❏ I plan my shopping and write out my list so I only have to go to the grocery store once every week or so.
6. ❏ Forget planning! I go to the store whenever I need something.

Total your check marks for 4 and 5. If you didn't check both of them, you are losing opportunities to save money through organized, systematic purchases.

Are you starting to see your food-buying profile? Now describe your food-buying habits more fully by answering the following questions:

When it comes to my food-buying skills, I _____

_____

_____

_____

When I'm really honest about it, I think that in order to save money on food I'll have to _____

_____

_____

Some shoppers believe that buying healthy, nutritious foods will cost them even more money, but that is not true, as we will see. Which of the following hinder or prevent you from buying more nutritious and/or less-expensive foods? Check all that apply, and feel free to add some of your own.

❏ Not enough time to prepare it.
❏ Lack of knowledge or interest in cooking.
❏ Limited buying options—no large grocery store nearby, or just one store nearby.
❏ Family members who will only eat certain foods.
❏ Can't afford to buy healthy, fresh foods.
❏ _____
❏ _____
❏ _____

Which changes might you be able to make in order to buy more nutritious and less-expensive foods?_____

_____

_____

If other people in your household also buy food, describe how your food-buying habits differ. _____

_____

_____

Who would be the better shopper for overall savings and quality of nutrition?

_____

Which changes might you want to make to your food-buying habits in light of your answers? _____

_____

_____

KNOW WHAT YOU ARE BUYING

One way to save money on food is to know what you are buying. If you're not familiar with basic nutritional needs and which combinations of foods make up a balanced meal, it's time to learn so you can get the best prices and receive the highest nutritional value for your dollar. The following suggestions can help you better understand the foods you buy.

Read Up on Nutrition

There are many sources of help for learning nutritional essentials, so if you're "hungry" to learn more, follow up on one or several of these resources.

- Family doctor, physician's assistant, or nurse practitioner
- County or city health department
- County extension service
- Local state community college, university, or adult education program
- Local public library
- U.S. Government Printing Office
- A knowledgeable neighbor, friend, or church or family member
- Community education programs offered by a local hospital
- Dietitian at a local hospital or residential facility

Which of these resources will you contact first? _____

Read the Labels

When you buy any kind of processed or prepared foods, know what you are buying.

✓ The labels on most foods reveal the ingredients and nutritional information. Compare such ingredients as salt, sugar, fat, additives, preservatives, calories per serving, net weight, etc. Usually ingredients are listed in descending order—the first ingredient is the predominant one, the last ingredient makes up the smallest portion of the product.

✓ Besides avoiding extra sugars (often disguised by such terms as sucrose, glucose, maltose, lactose, or corn syrup solids), be alert to levels of sodium and fat. Even if you are not on a low-sodium or fat-free diet, studies show that high levels of salt contribute to high blood pressure, and that high levels of fat, especially saturated fat, contribute to obesity and heart disease. Moderation is advised. Don't pay for ingredients you don't need or want.

✓ Learn all the names of any food additives that you want to avoid so you can make informed decisions about the prepared foods you buy. This is particularly important if members of your household have health conditions that require abstinence from certain substances.

Read the labels on several of your favorite foods. Which ingredients or quantities surprised you? _____

_____

Do you need to make some changes based on this new information? If so, what?

_____

_____

What food label information is of special importance to you? Percentage of fat? Amount of sugar? Food additives or coloring? _____

_____

When it comes to nutritional value and quality of food, feel free to ask questions. Many people do not make the best food purchases simply because they aren't willing to ask simple questions of the experts. A produce person can help you choose the best tomatoes for slicing, for flavoring salads, and for preparing a sauce; a butcher can help you choose cuts of meat that grill well. Admit what you don't know and have fun learning.

LEARN TO COMPARISON SHOP

In *Living Smart, Spending Less*, we discuss how much money you can save by visiting grocery stores in order to make your own comparisons according to your own needs and to draw conclusions according to your own criteria. Your neighbor, your best friend—even your mother—cannot do this for you. Why? Because no two people eat or buy food in exactly the same way.

If you have more than one option for the bulk of your food purchases, you'd be wise to comparison shop. It's not uncommon to find as much as a 15 percent difference in price on the same merchandise in different stores. For example, we have three major supermarket chains in our area. Most people think that chain "A" has the best prices. A few would say that chain "C" has the best prices. Through research, however, we discovered that chain "B" has the best prices and quality for the foods we buy. The key to savings is to determine which store(s) offer the foods you regularly buy at the lowest cost.

Do a Comparison Survey—and Save!

Use the following worksheets to survey the prices of the products you buy on a regular basis. (Feel free to photocopy these so you have plenty of them.) Survey prices in several stores, perhaps including stores in which you normally do not shop. In addition to supermarket chain stores, these stores may include a discount supermarket, independent supermarket, buying or warehouse club, and/or a restaurant supply house that sells to retail customers. You don't need to be exhaustive with this survey. Select three stores that you think have a good variety and reasonable prices, and see what you discover.

Hint: If a particular product is on sale when you do your survey, write down both the regular and the sale price. Indicate the sale price with a ☆ (star). This will help you know which stores offer deeper price cuts on sale merchandise.

Date of Survey:

Item: (specify size/quantity)	Store #1	Store #2	Store #3
Dairy Products:			
Milk:			
Eggs:			
Cheese:			
Butter/Margarine:			

	Store #1	Store #2	Store #3
Other:			
Meat Products:			
Hot/Cold Cereals:			
Fresh Fruit/Vegetables:			

	Store #1	Store #2	Store #3
Frozen Foods:			
Juice:			
Vegetables:			
Other:			
Breads:			
Baking Items:			
Flour:			
Sugar:			
Oil/Shortening:			
Mixes:			

	Store #1	Store #2	Store #3
Spices:			
Other:			
Canned Goods:			
Vegetables:			
Fruits:			
Condiments/Dressings:			
Soups:			

	Store #1	Store #2	Store #3
Bottled/Canned Beverages:			
Coffee/Tea:			
Juices:			
Water:			
Soda Pop:			
Dry Goods:			
Beans:			
Rice:			
Pasta:			
Other:			
Cookies/Crackers/Snacks:			

	Store #1	Store #2	Store #3
Paper Products:			
Cleaning/Laundry:			
Health/Beauty:			
Other: (Baby, Pet, etc.)			

Make the most of your survey results. Now it's time to compare the prices you've recorded. Calculate the total price for each store, then calculate the price for individual categories of products. Record your results below and check the store that offers the greatest savings.

Hint: Although the overall difference in price between different stores may be relatively low, the difference between certain categories of products may be significant.

○ Store 1: Total cost $_____
○ Store 2: Total cost $_____
○ Store 3: Total cost $_____

Dollar difference between lowest and highest price store? $_____

Product Category:	Store #1	Store #2	Store #3	High/Low Dollar Difference
Dairy Products				
Meat Products				
Hot/Cold Cereals				
Fresh Fruit/Vegetables				
Frozen Foods				
Breads				
Baking Items				
Canned Goods				
Bottled/Canned Beverages				
Dry Goods				
Cookies/Crackers/Snacks				
Paper Products				
Cleaning/Laundry				
Health/Beauty				
Other				

In what ways are you surprised by the survey results? _____
_____

Approximately how much could you save if you were willing to shop in the store that has the lowest prices for each category? _____

Is the savings you will achieve worth the extra effort required to shop in more than one store? _____

In what ways, on the basis of your survey results, will you change your shopping habits in order to save money on your food and household needs? _____
_____
_____
_____

Try to do this comparison shopping survey every six to nine months in order to keep up with changing trends in prices and quality. If the changes you note after several surveys are insignificant, consider doing the survey less frequently—perhaps every eighteen months or so.

Consider Other Shopping Options

In *Living Smart, Spending Less*, we evaluate five other shopping options: discount supermarkets, buying and warehouse clubs, restaurant supply houses (when buying in large sizes), home shopping plans, and buying cooperatives. Each alternative can provide major savings on grocery bills. Consult pages 166–168 for cautions and recommendations on shopping alternatives.

Where are the alternative shopping options in your area? List the names below.

Shopping Alternative

Discount supermarkets: 1. _____ 2. _____
                              3. _____

Buying and warehouse clubs: 1. _____ 2. _____

Restaurant supply houses: 1. _____ 2. _____

Home shopping plans: 1. _____ 2. _____
(Requires large freezer)

Co-ops: 1. _____ 2. _____

Which new food-buying options are you going to try? _____
_____
_____

How much do you anticipate you'll save? _____

ADDITIONAL WAYS TO SAVE MONEY ON FOOD

Even if you don't feel up to doing a full-scale price comparison like that described above, you can still save money on food. You can consider less-expensive alternatives to the foods you presently buy, you can buy on sale, you can guard against common costly errors, and you can care for what you buy so it doesn't go to waste.

Compare Prices Every Time You Shop

Comparison shopping is by no means limited to finding out which store has the best prices. Comparison shopping also means finding the least-expensive way to obtain the foods you need. Place a check mark in front of each shopping tip you will try the next time you shop. Then practice these strategies regularly.

❏ I will compare generic and house brands to name brands. (Different brands of food have different appearances and tastes, but the nutritional value generally is similar. Depending on your particular needs, a low-cost, generic brand may serve your purposes well.)

❏ I will compare the same sizes and amounts, so I am comparing "apples to apples."

❏ I will carry a small hand calculator to help in determining cost per ounce, pound, and/or item (vitamins) if such a figure is not already posted. (Beware of inaccuracies and inconsistencies in unit pricing. A small size may list a per-ounce unit price whereas the large size of the same item may list a per-pound unit price.)

❏ Before I buy a larger size or quantity, I will compare the prices of both smaller and larger sizes/quantities, realizing that not all large sizes are more economical than smaller sizes.

❏ I will use coupons to my advantage, but also with discretion. (Remember that most coupons are for prepared or highly processed convenience foods that are among the most expensive foods you can buy. You may save even more by purchasing the same type of food in a less-processed state.)

❏ I will compare convenience against cost. I recognize that convenience foods that have already received some degree of preparation that I could have done at home are typically more expensive than minimally processed foods. (Examples of more expensive convenience foods are: individually wrapped items, such as cheese slices, which cost much more than a whole unit of the same item; pre-measured and preseasoned packets of instant oatmeal compared with ready-to-cook oatmeal; frozen dinners compared with dinners you could prepare; and single-serving containers of yogurt, pudding, and fruit compared with the normal, packaged variety.)

❏ I will adopt several of the following ways to save money on the meat I buy.
   ❏ Buy whole chickens instead of cut-up ones.
   ❏ Buy meat with a lower percentage of bone and/or fat.
   ❏ Buy a whole ham and ask the butcher to slice it for me.
   ❏ Buy round steak on sale and have it ground up instead of buying regular ground beef.

❏ Buy whole turkeys on sale and freeze them.

❏ Go to an open market where I can buy fresh seafood as it comes off the boats (if it is less-expensive!).

❏ Compare the costs of processed meat (bacon, bologna, and so on) with other meat (a beef roast, a turkey, and so on), and buy unprocessed meat whenever possible.

Take Advantage of Sales

Sales often lower the cost of a particular item by as much as one-half to one-third. So if you shop carefully, you can cut your food bill significantly. Put a check mark in front of the following money-savers that you already use. Then put an X in front of the new ideas that will benefit you.

❏ Read the weekly supermarket advertisements in local newspapers and shop accordingly. Watch for "loss leaders" you'd buy anyway, which stores sell at or below their cost to attract customers. Also remember that not every item in a sales flyer is sale priced; some prices may be "everyday low prices."

❏ Stock up on staples that go on sale—if you have the pantry and/or freezer space to use them wisely.

❏ Plan menus around what's on sale and/or in season.

❏ If an item is "four for a dollar" only buy what you need; for instance, buy two for fifty cents if you need only two.

❏ Be willing to switch to a different brand if another brand of comparable quality goes on sale.

❏ Get a rain check from the store or department manager when the sale item(s) you want is sold out so you can buy the item(s) at the sale price when it is restocked. (And don't forget to use the rain check!)

❏ Watch for special markdowns. (We've purchased milk for $1.00 a gallon and meat at 75 percent off.) Often this happens when food must be sold by a specific date.

Avoid Common Shopping Mistakes That Cost You Money

No matter how much research you do, you may still make mistakes once you're inside a grocery store. Merchandisers use sophisticated techniques to entice you to buy impulsively. It pays to be on your guard so you don't fall prey to potentially expensive shopping practices.

As you read each of the following tips, rate yourself accordingly. Circling a "1" means you never apply the tip; a "5" means that you always use the tip. Then add up your scores at the end.

I generally do not buy nonfood items at the supermarket, choosing instead to buy them at discount stores.　　1 2 3 4 5

I enjoy "taste testing" foods in a grocery store but feel no obligation to buy what the salesperson is promoting.　　1 2 3 4 5

I purchase only the items on my shopping list—and leave without buying more.　　1 2 3 4 5

I scan items on lower shelves to see if the prices are lower on comparable quality merchandise than on the items on eye-level shelves.　　1 2 3 4 5

I don't buy impulse items I see when I first enter the store or items at the end of the aisles that look as if they're on sale but really aren't.　　1 2 3 4 5

I plan the meals ahead of time so I can save time and money when I shop.　　1 2 3 4 5

I don't shop when I'm in a hurry, tired, hungry, or otherwise not up to it.　　1 2 3 4 5

When I go in to buy a sale-priced item that's located near expensive foods, I only come home with the item I went into the store to buy.　　1 2 3 4 5

I think twice about buying specialty items—exotic fruit, "gourmet" snacks and cookies, "butcher-shop" meats, and specialty beverages.　　1 2 3 4 5

I think twice about buying high-priced cakes, cookies, soft drinks, and other goodies that are seldom healthy.　　1 2 3 4 5

I try to limit how much money I spend on "convenience" foods, preferring instead to buy less-processed foods.　　1 2 3 4 5

When I (and others who accompany me) stand in the check-out lane, I do not permit the candy, batteries, and magazines to snag undue attention (and my pocketbook).	1 2 3 4 5
At the check-out lane, I watch as the computer prints out the total for each item to ensure that I receive correct sale prices.	1 2 3 4 5
Anytime a product I purchase has less-than-expected quality, I return it to the store for a refund or substitution.	1 2 3 4 5
I watch for packages that have coupon and refund offers. Even in the same bin, not all the packages may be the same.	1 2 3 4 5

Now add your total score and see how well you did.

55-75	Saving quite a bit of money
35-54	Doing pretty well overall
34 and below	Room for significant improvement

Once the Food Is Home, Take Care of It

If you do a great job shopping but don't store the food properly, you'll lose some of the money you've worked hard to save. First, the food won't last as long or remain as nutritious. Second, you (and possibly others) might get sick and have to receive medical treatment. So take this opportunity to test your food transportation and storage skills. Check off the food-care tips you regularly practice:

- ☐ Do you store "bug-prone" dry staples (rice, flour, cereals, and so on) in sealed containers? (Grain-based foods, such as flour, may have bugs in them, so freeze them for a week or so before storing them.)
- ☐ Do you use leftovers wisely in order to stretch the food you buy?
- ☐ Do you keep meats, seafood, and poultry frozen until you need them and then thaw them only as long as necessary until they're ready for cooking?
- ☐ If you have a freezer and use it for long-term storage, have you set the thermostat for around 0 degrees Fahrenheit?
- ☐ Do you buy frozen and refrigerated foods last and, if it is a warm day, put them in a cooler before starting your trip home?

- [ ] If frozen foods have been partially thawed and then refrozen, do you use them as soon as possible?
- [ ] If the color or smell of a food item is bad when it's thawed, or a can is bulging or rusted, do you throw it out or return it to the store?
- [ ] Do you refrigerate thawed foods (especially meats, seafood, and poultry) and try to eat them as soon as possible, keeping the refrigerator at 40 degrees Fahrenheit?

Which new tip(s) will you put into use the next time you shop? _____

_____

_____

_____

9
Caring for a Car

Cars are the most convenient form of transportation: they are private, quick (except during rush-hour traffic jams), and can depart at any time. But they also are expensive. They require gas, oil, tires, regular maintenance, and at times require expensive repairs. Drivers have to pay for taxes, license fees, and insurance. (See the next chapter for insurance tips.) And people who lease or purchase cars on credit usually pay hundreds of dollars every month just to have a car.

But there are ways to reduce the expense of owning and operating a car. Maintaining your car the best you can—whether it's four weeks or four years old—will help keep it from wearing out and may prevent major repairs or an accident that could cost you thousands.

Financial Benefits of Regular Auto Maintenance

Although most of us use automobiles daily, it's easy to overlook their basic maintenance. Yet the benefits of regular auto maintenance can save far more money than many other money-saving things we do. Which of the following benefits of regular auto maintenance would you like to receive?

✓ Savings on fuel
✓ Increased safety

✓ Higher resale value

✓ Lower repair bills and fewer mechanical breakdowns

✓ Longer operating life

✓ Less pollution

✓ Fewer overall hassles with the car

With a commitment to planning ahead and maintaining your car before problems result, these benefits can be yours.

Choose the Repair Options That Fit Your Situation

It's helpful to realize two basic truths about car maintenance: 1. It's important that your car be maintained well, regardless of who does it. 2. If you car isn't maintained well, you'll pay more in auto-related expenses.

So how do you go about maintaining your car? Each of us has certain gifts and abilities. Perhaps you are great with a wrench. Perhaps you have never used one. Perhaps you love taking things apart. Perhaps you can never get things back together again. When it comes to maintaining your car, you have three options: 1. Learn when and how to do basic auto maintenance, and do it yourself. 2. Learn when maintenance is required, and either pay someone or ask a friend to do it for you. 3. Choose to know little or nothing about auto maintenance, and trust a repair shop or friend to do the work.

Your answers to the following questions will help you determine which of the above choices—or combination of choices—is best for you.

I ❑ would ❑ would not enjoy learning more about car maintenance.

I ❑ would ❑ would not enjoy even reading the car manual.

I ❑ would ❑ would not enjoy helping a friend maintain my car.

I ❑ would ❑ would not like to pay a shop to do maintenance I could learn to do myself.

I ❑ would ❑ would not be willing to trust a shop to do all the maintenance on my car.

I ❑ have ❑ do not have the money to pay a shop to maintain my car.

I ❑ have ❑ do not have a friend or family member who could help me learn basic car maintenance tips.

I ❑ would ❑ would not be able or willing to follow necessary safety procedures when working on my car.

I ❑ own ❑ have access to ❑ have no access to basic tools.

I ❑ tend to be patient ❑ am impatient when repairing things.

I ❑ have time ❑ do not have time to learn and do basic auto maintenance.

I ❑ am physically able ❑ am not physically able to do basic auto maintenance.

I ❑ live ❑ do not live in a setting where I could safely park and work on a car.

What did you learn about yourself and auto maintenance? Are you willing and able to learn basic maintenance skills? Would you rather pay a shop to do it all for you? Or are you somewhere in the middle? Even if you feel time and skills limit your involvement, there are several things you can do to make your car safer and drive it longer. Consider the maintenance requirements that are outlined in the following guide and determine how you will accomplish the remaining tasks.

CAR MAINTENANCE GUIDE

The following guide outlines car maintenance that will help maximize your car's life and minimize unexpected, expensive repairs. It supplements, but doesn't replace, the scheduled maintenance your car manufacturer recommends. Please don't neglect your manufacturer's instructions.

A symbol like this ◆ means you can probably do the maintenance yourself. A symbol like this ✳ means you'll probably need the help of a shop to complete the task. If you see both symbols, you may be able to do the task yourself but may prefer to have an experienced mechanic do the work, depending on your skill, confidence level, physical condition, the tools you have available, and so on. Notice how many tasks you can do yourself!

As with any responsible task, know your limitations. If you are not sure of how to do a specific task but really want to try it, ask a knowledgeable friend or a professional mechanic before you get started or as soon as you have a question or notice a problem. Or study a repair manual for your car. It's always better to be safe than sorry.

And speaking of being safe, always follow basic safety rules, such as not smoking when you work on your car, being cautious around hot or moving parts, jacking up the car properly, and making sure you use appropriate tools and parts.

Note: If you have a diesel or air-cooled engine, not all of the following tips will apply. Check with your mechanic to see which maintenance tips you should follow.

Tires

❑ Use an air-pressure gauge to keep tires properly inflated so they   ◆
will wear evenly, handle safely, and not reduce gas mileage.

❑ Replace a tire when the tread gets down to 1/16 of an inch.   ◆

❑ Monitor tire alignment, watching for uneven wear spots or poor   ◆
steering patterns. If you notice these, have a shop check and
adjust alignment, if necessary.

❑ Rotate tires according to the manufacturer's instructions to gain the longest tread life. ◆ or ✳

Check Shock Absorbers or Struts

❑ Test these by pushing down hard on each front and back fender. If the car continues to bounce after you stop pushing, they may need to be replaced. ◆

❑ Look at each shock absorber/strut to see if it's leaking oil. If so, have them replaced. ◆

Check the Oil Level Regularly, Adding as Needed

❑ Read the oil level on the dipstick when the car is parked on level ground. (If you just turned off the engine, wait a few minutes before checking the dipstick so the oil can flow back to its normal level in the crankcase.) ◆

❑ Slowly add the correct oil (see below) to the engine until the oil level is right. Check the dipstick to ensure you added the right amount; overfilling is harmful to the engine. ◆

❑ Learn which weight and specification of motor oil should be used in your car's engine—given your locale, driving conditions, and the manufacturer's recommendations. ◆

Change the Oil and Oil Filter Regularly

Oil lubricates moving parts, reduces noise, fights rust and corrosion, acts as a seal for internal engine parts, and carries dirt to the oil filter for removal. After a while, oil gets dirty and breaks down. By putting clean oil into the engine regularly, you can remove dirt particles before they damage the delicate insides of the engine. Many mechanics recommend that the oil and oil filter be changed about every 2,500 miles. Here are the steps you or your mechanic must perform to change the motor oil.

❑ Loosen the oil fill cap and remove the old oil filter. ◆ or ✳

❑ Remove the oil pan drain plug and allow the used oil to flow into a container for safe disposal. ◆ or ✳

❑ Tighten the drain plug to proper specifications after the old oil has been removed. ◆ or ✳

❑ Install a new oil filter, being careful to lubricate the gasket with fresh oil. ◆ or ✳

❑ Properly dispose of the used oil by taking it to a gas station or ◆ or ✳

other site that accepts used oil. (Even one gallon of oil that leaks into the earth at a landfill can taint the water supply.)

❑ Add the correct quantity of new oil, checking the dipstick as you do so. ◆ or ✳

❑ Tighten the oil fill cap, and run the engine for several minutes. Check for any oil leaks and recheck the oil level. ◆ or ✳

Caring for the Battery

❑ Be sure the battery terminals don't have a yellowish/whitish powder—acidic corrosion—on them. If they do, you'll need to apply the following steps to neutralize the corrosion. ◆

(1) Use a mixture of baking soda and water on an old rag or paper towels to wipe off the first layer of acidic corrosion that's on the terminals. Properly dispose of the rag or towels afterwards. (Be careful! The film and deposits on the outside of the battery are corrosive, so don't get them on your body, in your eyes, on your clothes, or even on the floor of your garage. Battery gases are explosive, so don't smoke or create sparks by allowing a metal object to touch both battery terminals at the same time.) ◆ or ✳

(2) Note which terminal is positive (+)—and negative (−). ◆

(3) Use a wrench to take the negative (−) terminal off the battery first and then take the positive (+) terminal off the battery. ◆

(4) Remove each terminal, and lightly sand it and the battery post with medium sandpaper until they both are shiny. (If you need to use more baking soda and water, do so in small quantities.) Then carefully wipe everything dry, put petroleum jelly (or anticorrosion rings that you buy at an auto parts store) on each terminal. ◆

(5) Carefully match the positive terminal with the positive battery post and firmly tighten the terminal back on the post. Then do the same with the negative terminal and post. If you become confused, ask a knowledgeable friend or professional mechanic before hooking things back up. ◆

❑ If your battery isn't sealed ("maintenance free"), gently remove the battery caps and make sure all the holes are filled with distilled water or cared for according to the battery's instructions. If you have questions about what to do, call the store where you bought the battery or a reputable mechanic. ◆

❑ Check the battery cables for corrosion, which can limit the flow of electricity from the battery. Replace them if necessary.   ◆ or ✳

Maintain Brakes Properly

Brakes are one of the most important parts of your car to maintain. Repairs for neglected brake systems can be expensive, and accidents caused by brake failure can be even more costly! The key to savings is to make sure brakes are monitored and cared for properly.

❑ Pay attention to unusual braking—either in pulling to one side   ◆
or the other, metal noises, or a brake pedal that's "mushy" or
goes to the floor. By catching problems early, you can prevent
or minimize expensive damage.

❑ If you notice any of the problems listed above, have your brake   ◆
system inspected immediately.

❑ Even if you experience no unusual brake symptoms, brakes   ◆ or ✳
need to be checked periodically for wear. Follow your
manufacturer's or mechanic's recommendations.

❑ The easy way to have your brakes inspected is to take the car   ◆ or ✳
into a brake shop that offers free brake checks. Or, learn how to
check the brakes yourself, wheel by wheel.

❑ Periodically check the brake fluid level in the master cylinder to   ◆ or ✳
be sure it's near the top. (The master cylinder uses the pressure
you put on the brake pedal to multiply the force so the brakes
work.) Be careful that no dirt enters when you remove the
cap(s). Add the correct type and amount of brake fluid rated
DOT (Department of Transportation) as needed. Note: If the
fluid level is more than half an inch from the top, there
probably is a leak in the system that needs immediate attention.

Caring for the Transmission

❑ Be alert for transmission danger signs. If you see a transmission   ◆
fluid leak or hear unusual noises as the engine shifts, have a
professional mechanic inspect the transmission.

❑ It is important to periodically check the transmission fluid level.   ◆
The correct procedure for doing this varies according to the
type of transmission and the age and make of your car, so follow
the manufacturer's recommendations exactly.

❑ If the transmission fluid level is low, add the proper type and ◆
amount of fluid. Be careful not to overfill the transmission,
because this can damage it. (You may find it helpful to use a
funnel when adding fluid.)

❑ Service the transmission periodically. If your car has an ◆ or ✳
automatic transmission, change the transmission fluid and filter
according to the service schedule in the owner's manual. If
your car has a manual transmission, the fluid needs to be
replaced according to the manufacturer's recommendations.

Keep Fittings and Other Parts Lubricated

Particularly if you drive an older vehicle, some fittings and parts need to be lubricated/greased regularly. (On newer vehicles, many parts that used to need lubrication are lifetime sealed and require no servicing.) Check your owner's manual or ask a mechanic to show you which fittings/parts need attention and to help you select the appropriate kind of grease or oil. There are many different lubricants suited for specific purposes (wheel bearings, transfer case, transmission, and so on). Using the wrong type of lubricant can be costly. Answer the following questions to help you determine if you should do your own lubrication.

❑ Am I physically able to crawl around under my vehicle?
❑ Do I have a garage or other suitable location in which to do this?
❑ Do I have the skill and confidence needed to lubricate/grease all of the
fittings/parts myself and to do so efficiently and safely?
❑ Am I better off having a mechanic/quick-lube shop do this work?

Replace the Air Filter Regularly

❑ When the air filter (that catches dust and dirt in the air that's ◆ or ✳
entering the engine) becomes dirty enough that you can't see
much light through it when you hold it up to a light source,
replace it with a new one designed for your car. (Note: Buy an
"extended life" filter that catches more dirt than a standard
filter. And if your engine has a wing nut on top of the air cleaner
housing, be careful not to overtighten it after you install the
new filter. You could damage the body of the carburetor.)

Keep an Eye on the Coolant Level and Its Potency

Unless you have an air-cooled engine, your engine needs proper coolant. You may be able to care for the cooling system yourself, but be careful. Most antifreezes are toxic, you could damage the engine if you put cold water into a hot engine, and the removal of a radiator cap from a hot radiator could cause you to be sprayed with boiling water or steam. And if you're not careful when you try to flush out the cooling system, you could end up with a fountain of water spouting out of the carburetor—which happened to a friend of ours.

If you're still eager to learn, there's much you can do yourself!

❑ Check the coolant level when the engine is cool. (If the engine ◆
has a plastic, jug-like container with radiator coolant in it, you
can check the level without removing the radiator cap.)

❑ Test the cold-protection strength of the radiator's antifreeze by ◆
using an inexpensive tester. If the engine isn't protected
enough, you'll need to replace the antifreeze or add more.

❑ Every year, or according to your car manufacturer's guidelines, ◆ or ✳
drain and flush out the cooling system according to proper
procedures and add new antifreeze. The proper mix of
antifreeze to water is usually fifty/fifty.

SAFETY TIP: If you spill any antifreeze, dilute it with water immediately and clean up what you can. Most types are poisonous, yet are tasty to many pets. You may want to switch to a nontoxic antifreeze.

Keep the Engine Tuned Up

This involves installing new spark plugs (and a condenser, distributor points, distributor cap, and rotor if your car doesn't have electronic ignition), and adjusting engine timing and the carburetor. Years ago, almost any backyard mechanic could do a tune-up. But today's newer cars are much more complicated and may require that a tune-up be done by a shop that has specialized equipment.

❑ Tune up your car according to the manufacturer's maintenance ◆ or ✳
schedule. If you notice a drop in fuel economy, experience
starting difficulties, or notice that the engine is not running
smoothly, you may need a tune-up before the recommended
interval.

Check the Exhaust System

❑ If you smell exhaust in the car, ventilate to bring in fresh air and ✳
have the system checked immediately. Deadly carbon

monoxide fumes, which have no odor or color, are one of the components of exhaust.

❑ Is the muffler getting louder or is an exhaust pipe hanging down? Have it repaired or replaced.   ✳

Care for the Car's Finish and Interior

❑ Wash and wax the car regularly. Be aware that some automatic car washes use "rough" rotating brushes that can damage the finish of your car.   ◆ or ✳

❑ If you live in an area where salt is put on the roads, wash and wax your car more often.   ◆

❑ Clean the interior as needed. Vacuum floors and upholstery, clean and condition vinyl, and don't forget to clean interior glass!   ◆ or ✳

❑ Park the car in a garage or carport—away from sun that fades, hail that dents, salt that rusts, tree sap that spots, and birds that show no respect.   ◆

❑ Park away from other cars, when you can, to reduce the risk of side-panel dings.   ◆

❑ Put in plastic and/or carpet floor mats to minimize wear and protect the floor from stains.   ◆

❑ Fix scratches in the finish quickly so exposed metal won't rust.   ◆ or ✳

Check the Condition of the Wiper Blades

❑ Are they streaking? Squeaking? Not clearing the water off the windshield? If so, replace the rubber blades. (Note: Some cars require a whole new wiper-arm assembly; others simply require replacement of the rubber blade.)   ◆ or ✳

Monitor the Windshield Wiper Fluid Reservoir

❑ Check the fluid level periodically, and add wiper fluid as needed to keep the reservoir full.   ◆

❑ During the winter months, make sure the fluid mixture is rated low enough for the temperatures in which you drive. Frozen fluid won't do you much good!   ◆

Periodic Maintenance

Four items to check periodically are belts and hoses, the fuel filter, power steering fluid level, and the air conditioning system. *Broken belts and leaky hoses* are among the most common causes of roadside breakdowns. By monitoring their condition and replacing them in a timely manner, you can reduce the chances of expensive on-the-road repairs. Tighten a belt that has more than half an inch of "give" in it when you push on it. Replace worn, cracked, and/or frayed belts, as well as a water hose that is leaky, swollen, and/or cracked or that has a soft spot in it.

You can change the *fuel filter* according to the manufacturer's recommendations. Similarly, inspect the power steering fluid level and add the proper type (according to your owner's manual) and amount. If you have *air conditioning*, have your repair shop maintain the system seasonally by charging it up, adjusting the compressor drive belt, and so on. Don't do this yourself; it can be quite dangerous. During the off-season, follow the manufacturer's recommendations for using the air conditioner.

SELF-MAINTENANCE CHECKLIST

As you have discovered, there are many routine maintenance tasks that are easy to do yourself. In fact, the most difficult part of some of them is to discipline yourself to do them! Newer auto owner's manuals have maintenance schedules with checklists. If your manual does not, prepare your own checklist. On a sheet of paper list each task shown above. Then across the top show the distance in 500 miles intervals: 500, 1,000, 1,500, 2,000, 2,500, 3,000, etc.

For each task, simply put an "X" in the box at the mileage point you determine to do the task. (Consult your owner's manual or mechanic if you have any questions about how frequently you should perform a task.) If you do not plan to do some of the tasks listed yourself, make sure your repair shop completes the necessary service instead. When your odometer reaches 500 miles, do the tasks marked on the chart, and continue the pattern for each additional 500 miles you drive. When you reach 5,000 miles, repeat the cycle.

MONEY-SAVING AUTO TIPS

Performing routine maintenance in a timely manner is one way to save money on automobile operating costs, but it isn't the only way. There are also ways to save money on your fuel costs and to minimize the cost of the repairs your car will need.

Fuel-Savings Tips

Check off the tips you regularly use, and star the ones you want to try.

❑ Buy the gasoline your car is designed to use. If you're not sure which octane rating your engine requires, check the owner's manual or ask a dealer who sells your make of car. There's no point in paying for extra octane your car doesn't need.

❑ If the engine makes a rapping sound or "knock," particularly when accelerating, purchase the next higher octane.

❑ Try different brands of fuel to see which one(s) works best for your car and driving needs.

❑ Don't let the engine idle for longer than a minute. It requires less gasoline to restart an engine than to let it idle for longer than a minute.

❑ "Warming up" the car for an extended period of time consumes fuel unnecessarily. Today's motor oils are designed to protect the engine when it's cold, so only a short warm-up is needed in cold weather.

❑ Accelerate smoothly to increase gas mileage and reduce engine wear.

❑ If the car has a manual transmission, don't "wind up" the engine higher than necessary. You'll keep the engine running at a slower speed, which will save gas and reduce engine wear. (But a mechanic also advises not to lug the engine by shifting at too low a speed because that's hard on engine bearings.)

❑ Whenever possible, keep windows closed when you drive. (Open windows create air resistance, which reduces gas mileage.)

❑ Drive at fifty-five miles per hour instead of sixty-five. The average car uses 17 percent less gasoline at fifty-five than at sixty-five.

❑ Combine errands in logical order so you drive fewer overall miles and allow your engine to warm up fully so it will run more efficiently.

❑ Do your initial shopping by phone. Once you know which store has what you need at the price you want to pay, then drive there.

❑ Minimize fast starts, hard stops, and constant lane changing.

❑ Join a carpool or take public transportation to work.

❑ Take advantage of cash-discounts gas stations when buying gas.

❑ Monitor your car's gas mileage regularly and investigate sudden drops in mileage promptly.

❑ Shop at businesses that offer free or inexpensive delivery, if their quality and prices are comparable to others.

❑ Buy a locking gas cap if your car doesn't have one. When times get hard, some people siphon gas from other people's cars.

❑ Keep the engine tuned up and the carburetor adjusted properly.

❑ If the engine is idling at too high a rate, have it adjusted.

❑ Don't "race" the engine when you first start it. This wastes fuel and also puts unnecessary stress and wear on the engine.

Noticing Car Problems Early

It is important to learn your vehicle's idiosyncrasies. If it starts operating differently, take note and investigate. By paying attention to your car's sights and sounds and responding quickly, you'll be able to reduce repair costs and avoid some inconvenient breakdowns. In order to avoid trouble, never ignore these warning signs:

- ✓ A dashboard warning light comes on.
- ✓ You feel unusual vibrations.
- ✓ A fluid of some kind is puddling underneath the vehicle.
- ✓ You hear unusual noises in the engine, rear end, or brakes.
- ✓ You smell something odd (oil, steam, grease, antifreeze, burned rubber).
- ✓ You hear a funny clunk when you put the car into gear.
- ✓ The engine is "missing"—just isn't running smoothly.
- ✓ The engine isn't starting or warming up properly.
- ✓ The fan belt is squealing.
- ✓ You hear a "growling" noise from where the radiator fan is. (The water pump may be going bad.)
- ✓ A distinct smell of gasoline is present. (Don't operate the car.)
- ✓ You can hear a hissing noise when the engine is running. (A vacuum line may be detached.)
- ✓ You see steam coming out from under the hood.
- ✓ Your lights suddenly get dim, or the battery will hardly start the car.
- ✓ You hear squealing or growling noises when you turn the steering wheel. (The power steering pump may be low on fluid or going bad.)
- ✓ The clutch is grabbing, chattering, or otherwise not working properly.

Which, if any, of these warning signs is your vehicle showing?_____
_____

What are you going to do about it? _____
_____

Reducing On-the-Road Repairs

- ▲ During a long trip, give someone other than the driver a spare set of keys. (Sure is cheaper than calling a locksmith.)
- ▲ Learn how to change a tire safely so you don't have to pay for emergency tire service.

▲ Always keep a few spare fuses in the sizes your car requires. (Many cars have places in the fuse box to store spare fuses.)

▲ Purchase a set of battery cables and learn how to use them properly. A quick "jump" can often get you out of a difficult situation without the expense and delay of an emergency service call.

Save Money on Routine Auto Parts

✓ Buy auto parts you use routinely (oil filters, oil, and so on) when they go on sale.

✓ Shop for tires carefully. Compare ratings, warranties, prices, mounting and balancing costs, cost difference between whitewalls and blackwalls, and so on.

✓ Consider joining a warehouse club to save money on tires, batteries, automotive tools, and supplies.

FINAL QUESTIONS

Who do you know who can help you learn to take better care of your car? (A mechanic? A friend? A family member?) _____

What are the advantages of paying close attention to what your vehicle is telling you? _____
_____

How much money do you think you may save by doing routine maintenance, listening to your vehicle's early warning signs, or simply by being prepared for on-the-road emergencies? _____

10
Saving a Bundle on Car Insurance

Buying insurance is a bit like carrying a first-aid kit when you go hiking. For years you may never even need it. Then one day, in an emergency, many of the items you've carried around for so long—various bandages, ointment, scissors, and so on—will be invaluable and could even save a life. Insurance coverage, along with savings and investments, plays a vital role in preserving your assets, so it's very important that you select the right insurance company and the coverage that you need.

EVALUATE THE TYPES AND AMOUNTS OF COVERAGE YOU HAVE

Because your insurance needs may be quite different from someone else's, it's important to determine what your needs are. Take a moment now and pull out your car insurance policy. Consider the amounts and types of coverage you currently have.

✓ Property Damage and Bodily Injury Liability Coverage

This coverage protects your assets because it will pay for damage your vehicle does to others and their property for which you are liable. Depending on where you live, you may be required by law to carry liability insurance. Given the high cost of medical care and the money that juries sometimes award accident victims, it pays to have adequate liability coverage.

Often liability coverage is described by three numbers. The company insuring a person who has 100/250/100 coverage will pay up to $100,000 to any one person injured in a single automobile accident, a maximum of $250,000 for total bodily injuries when more than one person is injured in an accident, and up to $100,000 per accident for property damage.

What amounts of liability coverage do you presently carry? _____

_____

Given your financial situation, are those amounts adequate? If not, what should they be? (Your insurance agent should be able to help you determine this.) _____

_____

✓ Collision Coverage
_____

If your car collides with another object or turns over, collision coverage pays for the repairs.

What is the actual cash value of your car? $_____ (Check your local library, car dealer, or bank auto loan department to find out the *N.A.D.A.* (Blue Book) *Used Car Guide* retail value for cars of the same make, model, year, and equipment as yours. This is generally the standard by which actual cash value is determined.)

If you carry collision coverage, what is your deductible (the amount you have to pay on a claim before the insurance company begins to pay)? $_____

What is your annual premium for this coverage? $_____

NOTE: Since an insurance company will only pay up to the actual cash value of the car, consider dropping this coverage if your car is worth less than $2,200, or if your financial situation is such that you could absorb the loss. Use the money you'll save on premiums toward a future car purchase.

Another way to determine whether you should continue this coverage is to subtract your deductible from your vehicle's actual cash value. This figure is the maximum amount your insurance company would pay on a claim. Is this amount of coverage worth the premium cost? _____

✓ Comprehensive Coverage
_____

Comprehensive pays for theft and damage to your car caused by something other than a collision, including fire, vandalism, hail, flying rocks, or windstorms. The car's actual cash value is the maximum amount that will be paid for such damage, so you might consider dropping this coverage if you have an older vehicle (unless it's a valuable antique).

If you carry this coverage, what is your deductible? $_____

What is your annual premium for this coverage? $_____

Again, subtract your deductible from your vehicle's actual cash value to determine the maximum amount your insurance company would pay on a claim. Is this amount of coverage worth the premium cost? _____

✓ Uninsured/Underinsured Motorist Coverage

If another driver who injures you or a family member has no insurance, doesn't have enough insurance, or flees the accident scene and can't be located, this coverage pays for the medical bills related to the injuries. In some states, this coverage is required.

What is the amount of your uninsured motorist coverage? $_____

Determine, with the help of your agent, if this amount of coverage is adequate. If not, what should it be? _____

✓ Medical Payments Coverage

This pays the medical bills for you and/or your passengers if injury occurs while in, entering, or leaving your car—no matter who is at fault. It can cover such costs as funeral expenses and lost wages, too. Your insurance company pays these costs without your having to prove that the other party involved was at fault.

What is the amount of your medical payments coverage? $_____

Determine, with the help of your agent, if this amount of coverage is adequate. If not, what should it be? $_____

Other Coverages

Some states require "no-fault" insurance, which pays for your injuries and perhaps the injuries of your passenger(s) sustained in an auto accident (up to the policy limits) regardless of who is at fault. Designed to eliminate expensive, ongoing lawsuits to find out who was at fault in an accident, this coverage will pay for such losses as medical and hospital expenses and loss of income. It also covers any person driving your car with your permission but does not cover damage to vehicles. Not every state has a no-fault coverage law, so check with an insurance agent or state insurance official to determine what your insurance needs are.

Other coverages may be available or required in your state. These may include additional personal injury protection, towing, etc. Work with your agent to determine what type and amount of additional coverage you need. List additional coverages and any questions you want to ask your agent related to those coverages here:

1. _____
2. _____
3. _____

Once you have evaluated your insurance coverage and needs, it's time to select the policy and company that is best for you.

COMPARE COVERAGE AND COST

Auto insurance costs are rising, for many reasons. So it pays to save what you can on auto insurance. Whether you are shopping for a policy for the first time or comparing your existing policy to new price/coverage quotations from other companies, make sure you're getting the best deal for your money.

Chart Your Automobile Coverage

In order to compare car insurance coverage, you must know how much coverage you're carrying on each vehicle, what the deductibles are, and how much the coverage costs. Using your existing insurance policy as a guide, fill in the following chart. If you have more than three insured vehicles, simply extend the chart. To compare coverage and costs between companies, make additional copies of this chart. Use one copy to record your existing coverage and additional copies to record costs for each company from which you request bids.

Name of Company: Date:

Name of Agent: Phone:

Type and Amount of Coverage:	Deductible/Premium Cost:		
	Vehicle #1	Vehicle #2	Vehicle #3
Property Damage/Bodily Injury Liability:			
$$ to any one person injured in a single accident—$			
Maximum $$ for total injuries when more than one is injured—$			
$$ of property damage per accident—$			
Collision:			

Comprehensive:			
Uninsured/Underinsured Motorist: $			
Medical Payments: $			
Other:			
TOTAL AMOUNT OF PREMIUM			

To receive the greatest benefit from this chart, follow these suggestions:

❏ Use the chart to compare premium and coverage quotations from at least three insurance companies. They aren't all alike! Only compare financially strong companies that are listed favorably (A-plus or higher rating) by A. M. Best Company, Moody's Investors Service, Inc., and/or Standard & Poor's Corporation. You can find these rating guides in most public libraries.

❏ The company that has the lowest premium price may not always save you the most money. Select a company that pays its claims promptly, has knowledgeable and reliable agents, and has a good reputation. A company that doesn't pay its claims isn't a good choice, no matter how low the premiums are.

❏ Remember, the "biggest" company isn't necessarily "best." Some smaller companies do an excellent job.

❏ Once you've selected several companies that have favorable ratings, call their respective local agents. Talk to them about your insurance needs and compare coverages and prices over the phone. Make sure you use the same deductibles and coverage limits with each agent so the quotes you receive will be truly comparable. Sometimes agents give inaccurate or incomplete figures over the phone, so ask them to send you written quotes, too.

❏ Write down every quote on your insurance coverage chart so you can easily compare cost differences between companies.

CHOOSE A POLICY

Now that you know the comparative cost of your auto insurance, you're well on your way to choosing a money-saving policy. But before you make your final decision, it's important to consider the following money-saving tips:

❏ Choose the highest deductible you can afford in order to reduce your premium cost. (If you can afford to pay the first $500 of a claim, for example, compare the premium cost of a $500 deductible versus that of a $250 deductible.)

❏ Consider having higher collision and comprehensive deductibles on a new vehicle and dropping all comprehensive and collision insurance on older vehicles (except for antique vehicles).

❏ Be sure to carry enough insurance for your situation. (If you have quite a few assets, you'll want more protection because a plaintiff may sue you.)

❏ See how much it will cost to increase your liability coverage. (It may not be much in light of the extra protection you'll obtain.)

❏ Consider policies carefully. If you don't understand something, ask questions. Know what the policy will cover—and what it won't.

❏ Don't be in a hurry. An additional call could save you as much as 50 percent on your insurance premiums.

❏ If you do switch companies, keep the old policy in force until the new one takes effect. Don't risk a lapse in coverage.

❏ If you've been turned down by a few companies, for whatever reason, keep looking for a good one. Don't be sucked in by a "we can insure anyone" company.

❏ After you choose a company, check the insurance rating guides in the library annually and get quotes from other companies. Even a highly rated company can change its practices or become insolvent quickly.

❏ Evaluate premium payment options. Paying your premium annually instead of monthly, quarterly, or semiannually can save you money.

❏ Talk with your insurance agent from time to time about new coverages or available discounts.

❏ Request insurance-related information from the Better Business Bureau in your area and the state insurance commissioner's office.

MAXIMUM SAVINGS

Saving money on car insurance means more than simply finding the right policy. Don't overlook these ideas that can lead to even greater savings.

If You're Buying a New Car . . .

Inquire about insurance rates before you sign on the dotted line. Certain makes and models of cars are cheaper to repair or safer than others. So before you buy a car, check with your insurance company to see how much you'll have to pay to insure it. You may be surprised by what you learn. For example, did you know that:

☆ There may be a hundred dollars or more difference in annual premiums on very similar cars?

☆ Four-wheel-drive vehicles may be significantly more expensive to insure than two-wheel-drives?

☆ Premiums may even differ on the same make and model of car, depending on where it was assembled?

Are You Eligible for a Discount?

You may qualify for a discount on your insurance premium if you fit one or more of the following criteria. Put a check mark in any box that might apply, and then ask your insurance agent for details. These savings can add up!

❏ Do you have a clean driving record—no accidents or moving violations?

❏ Does your young driver earn good grades?

❏ Has your young driver completed a driver education course?

❏ Do you carpool?

❏ Do you commute fewer miles or less often than you did previously?

❏ Do you ride public transportation to work?

❏ Do you insure two or more cars with the same company?

❏ Are you a nondrinker or nonsmoker?

❏ Have you installed an antitheft device? Etched your vehicle windows?

❏ Does your car have antilock brakes, automatic seat belts, and/or an air bag(s)?

❏ Are you a senior citizen?

❏ Are you a woman over thirty who hasn't had an accident?

❏ Have you recently moved? Ask whether rates in the new area are lower.

Stand Up for Your Rights

Sometimes even a good company may not treat you in the way you think is fair. The following questions will help you determine what your options may be if you and an insurance company disagree.

Would you feel comfortable talking over a problem with your insurance agent or an insurance company representative assigned to your case? (Note: This is generally the best place to start.) Why or why not?_____

_____

_____

_____

Write down the address of your state's insurance commissioner's office so you can write them a letter that factually documents your case if talking with the agent or representative doesn't solve anything. _____

_____

Would you ever be willing to accept a settlement you think is unfair? Why or why not? _____

Are you willing to consult a lawyer who will guide you through insurance issues and legal potholes? (Note: This can be especially important after a car accident.) Why or why not? _____

_____

Which person(s) can you talk with if you need wisdom concerning a car insurance –related problem? _____

_____

_____

_____

11
Reduce the Expense of Flying

Although most of us travel by car, an increasing number also travel by plane. In fact, nearly eight million people in the United States each week board a regularly scheduled airplane.[1] You may be one of them. Air travel can be expensive due to fuel costs and a complex rate structure. But there are many ways to save. The following proven tips aren't all-inclusive; such a list would take up a whole book. But you can use them to better understand how the airlines work and save money on future trips.

THE HELPFUL TRAVEL AGENT

The trick to air travel savings is to find out which airline, fare, and schedule will give you the greatest value for the dollars you spend. And with the help of a good travel agent, you don't even have to do the work of finding the lowest fares yourself. Your agent can do the work for you.

Review the following benefits that a travel agent can provide. Rank them in order of importance to you. Feel free to add other benefits, if you desire.

❑ You save time by not having to check prices and schedules yourself.
❑ You quickly learn about scheduling options and can easily arrange convenient schedules.
❑ You get the most for your travel dollars.

- ❑ You can use the agent's expertise in other travel-related areas, such as cruises, car rentals, hotel reservations, and/or tour packages.
- ❑ You receive these services free, because the agent is paid on commission by the airlines and other travel-service providers.
- ❑ You have the assurance that your agent will back you up if a problem develops.
- ❑ You can have your ticket(s) delivered to you.
- ❑ _____
- ❑ _____

If you aren't presently using a travel agent, why aren't you? _____
_____
_____

Select the Right Agent

Some travel agents are better than others. The following checklist will help you evaluate agents and agencies as you search for a competent and personable travel agent. If you already have a travel agent, it will help you know when it's time to find a different one.

- ❑ Which agents do your friends, family members, and/or business associates recommend? _____
_____
_____

- ❑ Give three "recommended" travel agents exactly the same information regarding an upcoming trip. Tell them when you'd like to travel and where you plan to go. Tell them you'd like to go the cheapest way possible and find out which options could save you money. Then compare the scheduling and pricing information you receive from each.
- ❑ Ask each agent if he/she will notify you of promotional fares or rate changes that might benefit you.
- ❑ Be willing to try an out-of-town agency that uses a toll-free line.
- ❑ Notice which agent returns your phone calls promptly.
- ❑ Notice which agent understands your desire to obtain the best schedule for the least amount of money. (Remember, an agent who finds you the lowest fare works hard and receives less money for doing so.)

LEARN HOW TO PAY LESS FOR AIRLINE TICKETS

Whenever possible, try not to pay full fare for airline tickets. Which of the following methods have you used to reduce the cost of flying? Put a check mark in front of each that you have used. If you encounter new suggestions, take note of them so you can apply them the next time you purchase airline tickets.

❑ I determine my travel schedules and make reservations through my travel agent well in advance so I can meet purchase restrictions on the best fares.

❑ I ask my travel agent to promptly inform me of promotional fares that might benefit me so that I can make reservations before the limited number of fares sell out.

❑ When I have to make last-minute travel plans and may have to pay full fare, I request a waiver from advance-purchase restrictions so I can fly more cheaply. (The airline may agree to this if seats on the plane will remain unsold otherwise.)

❑ I consider buying an annual air pass for domestic travel. (If you qualify to use a pass, compare the air pass's rules, restrictions, and prices from airline to airline. Do the benefits outweigh the cost and the restrictions when compared to buying individual tickets?

❑ When I buy advance tickets and the prices go down between the time of purchase and the time of departure, I ask my agent (or the airline counter agent when I check in for the flight) if I am eligible for a refund of the difference between the two fares or if the tickets can be reissued at the lower fare.

❑ I consult my travel agent to compare travel packages that combine air travel with other arrangements. (This often saves money, but always ask about any restrictions, hidden fees, occupancy requirements, and so on.)

❑ When I plan to fly one way, I consider buying a round-trip ticket if it costs less and not use the return portion. (Some people have an ethical problem with this practice. Use your own judgment.)

❑ I read the Sunday newspaper and listen to radio and television ads to find out about special airline promotions—including introductory fares—and to find special discount coupons. (Read the fine print to learn about restrictions, hidden fees, hidden package costs, and so on.)

❑ I request that the airline grant me a lower fare or waive advance-purchase restrictions if I need to attend a funeral for a family member or be with someone during an emergency. (You may need documentation to prove that the emergency is real. A signed letter or fax from your doctor or the telephone of someone who can verify the situation often is sufficient.)

THE VALUE OF FLEXIBILITY

If you're serious about saving money, flexibility is essential. We have flown on different airlines, changed our flight times at the last minute, flown to alternate cities close to our destination, and returned home earlier or later than we'd first planned in order to maximize our savings. As you do your trip planning, determine which of the following money-saving tips you are able and willing to do.

❑ Check in and get a boarding pass early—at least an hour before scheduled departure—to minimize your chances of being "bumped."

❑ Stay over a Saturday night in your destination locale if that qualifies you for cheaper tickets. The money you save will more than cover the cost of an overnight hotel stay.

❑ Travel on late-night or early-morning flights when your schedule allows.

❑ Travel during the off-season when fares may be lower and there may be fewer people traveling.

❑ Leave or return on key holidays when fewer people travel. (You may get a reduced fare because the airline wants to fill more seats.)

❑ Be willing to fly through an airline's hub instead of flying nonstop.

❑ Fly on a smaller carrier if the fare is cheaper.

❑ Travel during the middle of the week if an airline wants to fill empty seats and lowers prices accordingly.

❑ Enroll in frequent-flyer programs. Why not receive free tickets as a reward for flying—plus obtain special fares, discount coupons, bonus mileage, hotel discounts, and so on! Rules, conditions, and benefits change regularly, so compare programs carefully.

❑ If you're flying to several cities, check the lowest fare to each one and be flexible about the order in which you visit the cities on your itinerary. You may, for example, save money by flying to the farthest city first. Or you may fly into one city on a major airline and then transfer to a different airline for the last leg of your trip—all for one fare.

❑ Agree to be "bumped" off a flight if:
  (1) the airline will offer you a free ticket or ticket voucher that has restrictions you can live with;
  (2) you will have a good chance of catching a later plane—perhaps even a guaranteed seat on the next available flight; and
  (3) you have carry-on luggage and aren't in a hurry.

❑ Competition between certain cities and routes keeps some air fares low. You can use competition to your advantage if you:
  (1) Fly into an alternate airport near your destination when the fare is significantly lower and you have transportation to your final destination (a friend who picks you up, public transportation, and so on).

(2) Are willing to fly a different, competitive route that may involve a longer flight time or plane change.

IN CASE OF PROBLEMS

If you travel, you will eventually experience hassles. Some, like weather-related delays, are like the law of gravity—they'll keep happening no matter what. Other travel problems can be avoided. Some travel problems are of little financial consequence. Others can be expensive. Consider each of the following tips that could save you money in a crisis. Mark the ideas that are new to you so you can remember them for your next trip.

- ✓ Pay by credit card if an airline you fly has filed for protection from creditors. This will give you recourse to a refund, subject to certain limitations, if the airline stops flying.
- ✓ Treat each ticket like the cash it represents. If someone else uses your ticket, you're out of luck. If it's lost or stolen, you may have to buy another at full fare (but always ask the airline to waive the advance-purchase requirement on the new ticket and permit you to purchase it at a reduced fare). If a ticket is lost or stolen, you may need to apply for a refund, which can take a long time and cost you a fee.
- ✓ If you miss a flight due to your error, apologize to the ticket agent and ask to be put on standby status for the next available flight to your destination.
- ✓ If you have a confirmed reservation for a flight, you checked in at least thirty minutes prior to departure, and the airline "bumps" you because they over-booked, you're entitled to compensation. That may include guaranteed seating on the next flight, vouchers for future tickets, or overnight accommodations. Procedures vary, so you will avoid problems if you know your rights as a passenger on each airline.
- ✓ If your flight is delayed and you miss a connecting flight too late in the day to catch another one, the airline must: put you up at a hotel and arrange for your transportation the next morning; charter a van and drive you to your destination; or pay the cost of a rental car.
- ✓ If you become sick or injured and can't use your nonrefundable ticket, ask your doctor to document that in a letter. In most instances, you'll receive a refund.
- ✓ If something other than an emergency prevents you from using a ticket, contact your travel agent or the airline's customer service office to try to reschedule your flight. (It's easier to reschedule than to obtain a refund.)

How many money-saving tips did you learn? _____ Don't forget them!

1. Based on 1991 domestic passenger-boarding statistics of 412,269,000 people, provided by the Air Transport Association, 1301 Pennsylvania Ave., N.W., Washington, DC 20004.

12
Enjoy the Benefits of a Spending Plan

While holding a glass of milk during a meal, Stephen felt something dripping onto his lap. Surprised, knowing the glass was upright, he looked around to see what else had spilled. Nothing had. Then he turned the glass around and discovered a small hole. He plugged the leak with his finger until he got a different glass.

In a similar way, each of us needs to plug small and large "money leaks" that drain us financially. A wise spending plan (or budget, as it is more commonly called) will guide you in allocating money wisely so you can plug money leaks, take steps to reduce your debt, and make the most of your finances.

WHAT ARE THE ADVANTAGES OF A SPENDING PLAN?

Hmm . . . a spending plan. Sounds like a disguised budget, you may be thinking. *Why should I bother to take the time to do it?*

Some people view a spending plan as a whip-cracking slave driver that pushes them in directions they don't want to go. To them, a spending plan is to be avoided at any cost. Let's assume, however, that a properly used spending plan can lead to great rewards. What might those rewards be? How do you know if a spending plan can help you? Quiz yourself using the following questions—and read on!

	YES	NO
Are you fully aware of how you (and your spouse) spend money so you can accurately reduce or eliminate unnecessary spending?		
Do you know what percentage of your income is spent on expenses?		
Are you prepared for lean economic times?		
Might there be ways in which you can use your current and estimated income more effectively?		
Would you like more accurate information concerning your finances so you can make wise choices, meet needs, satisfy wants, and attain desired goals?		
Would you appreciate having a way to measure your progress in saving money and reducing unnecessary spending?		
Would you like to improve your future standard of living?		
Would it be helpful to have a base from which to discuss financial goals with your family and/or friends?		
Do you want to have more money available for investments and charitable giving?		
Do you want to reduce your personal debt—or eliminate it?		
Do you know what percentage of your income is spent on expenses?		
Do you want to have the resources to take advantage of true bargains?		
Would you like to see others, including family members, become motivated to participate in the saving process?		

If you answered yes to most or all of these questions, a spending plan will be quite helpful to you. The process outlined in this chapter is designed to prepare you to develop a workable spending plan. The first step is to take inventory of your existing financial situation and spending habits. On the basis of that information, you can then evaluate your expenses and income and make the short- and long-term adjustments necessary to accomplish your financial goals.

It's true that developing and living by a spending plan is not as much fun initially as spending money any way you want to. However, over time, a good spending plan can give you much greater financial opportunities. It can be written in a day or two. But a spending plan can only work for you if you put it into practice.

Note: To make this process easier, before you begin make several copies of the worksheets in this chapter. You will use the expense and income worksheets to record your spending history and to outline your spending plan. From time to time, you will also want to update your spending plan and reassess your assets and liabilities. Additional copies of the worksheets will make this task easier.

LIST YOUR ASSETS AND LIABILITIES

This is an important step in developing a spending plan. As you list your assets (the financial value of what you own) and your liabilities (the money you owe through consumer debt, home mortgage, taxes, pledges, and so on), you will begin to see what your financial picture really looks like. *It's very important to be as accurate as possible.* If you are married, and you each own things separately, initial which assets are owned by whom. If you happen to own a number of assets, you may need to list them on a separate sheet and simply add the total to this worksheet.

We will divide the assets into two categories: *liquid,* which can be converted to cash easily, and *nonliquid,* which may take time to convert to cash.

ASSETS

LIQUID ASSETS:

Use the following worksheets to list your liquid assets. Write down today's cash value and be as accurate as you can. If you need more room, use a separate sheet of paper.

Savings and/or Money Market Account(s):
- ❏ Financial institution:_____ $_____
- ❏ Financial institution:_____ $_____
- ❏ Financial institution:_____ $_____
- ❏ Financial institution:_____ $_____
- ❏ Financial institution:_____ $_____

Checking Account(s):
- ❏ Financial institution:_____ $_____
- ❏ Financial institution:_____ $_____
- ❏ Financial institution:_____ $_____
- ❏ Financial institution:_____ $_____

Cash on Hand: $_____

Marketable Securities (today's cash value): $_____

❑ Financial institution:_____ $_____
❑ Financial institution:_____ $_____
❑ Financial institution:_____ $_____

Bonds (today's cash value):

❑ _____ $_____
❑ _____ $_____
❑ _____ $_____

Stocks (today's cash value):

❑ _____ $_____
❑ _____ $_____
❑ _____ $_____

Mutual Funds (today's cash value):

❑ _____ $_____
❑ _____ $_____
❑ _____ $_____

Certificate(s) of Deposit (maturity date):

❑ _____ $_____
❑ _____ $_____
❑ _____ $_____
❑ _____ $_____

Insurance Policy/Policies (cash value):

❑ _____ $_____
❑ _____ $_____
❑ _____ $_____

TOTAL LIQUID ASSETS **$_____**

NONLIQUID ASSETS:

Value of Appraised Collection(s):
(Stamps, antiques, coins, etc.)

❏ _____ $_____

❏ _____ $_____

❏ _____ $_____

IRA/Keogh Funds:

❏ _____ $_____

❏ _____ $_____

❏ _____ $_____

Pension/Profit-sharing Plan(s):

❏ _____ $_____

❏ _____ $_____

❏ _____ $_____

Real Estate (current value):

❏ Home_____ $_____

❏ Land_____ $_____

Other Real Estate Investments:

❏ _____ $_____

❏ _____ $_____

Personal Debts Owed to You:

❏ Person(s)_____ $_____

❏ Person(s)_____ $_____

❏ Person(s)_____ $_____

Business Debts Owed to You:

❏ Business_____ $_____

❏ Business_____ $_____

Business Valuation:

❏ Value of shares in one or more businesses _____ $_____

❏ _____ $_____

Limited Partnership(s):

❏ _____ $_____

Value of Personal Property (Use current resale value):

- ❑ Automobile(s) $_____
- ❑ Camper, boat, etc. $_____
- ❑ Appliances $_____
- ❑ Furniture $_____
- ❑ Jewelry $_____
- ❑ _____ $_____
- ❑ _____ $_____
- ❑ _____ $_____

TOTAL NONLIQUID ASSETS $_____

LIABILITIES

Now list your liabilities: the money that you owe and the financial terms. Your creditors may include: credit card companies, the bank (auto, furniture, boat loans), the mortgage company (money left on your mortgage), your parents, a former business partner, a Christian organization you've promised to support, an individual who loaned you money, a life insurance company, and so on. Again, be as accurate as possible. If you need more room, use a separate sheet of paper and transfer totals here.

Type of Debt/ Name of Creditor	Balance Due	Monthly Payment	Loan Length	Interest Rate
Mortgage				
Auto Loan				
Education Loan				
Personal Loans				
Business Loan(s)				
Investment Debt				
Pledges				

Other				
Total Liabilities				

Determine Your Net Worth

Add your Liquid and Nonliquid Assets together to find your total
assets: $_____

Subtract your Total Liabilities: $_____

The difference between your Assets and Liabilities is your Net Worth $_____

Were you surprised to find out what your net worth really is? _____ Why?
In what ways did you expect it to be different? _____

_____

_____

What have you learned about your financial condition by listing your assets and liabilities and determining your net worth?_____

_____

_____

In light of this new information, what changes in your financial situation do you
want to make? _____

_____

_____

DETERMINE YOUR ANNUAL EXPENSES

Another key to unlocking your financial puzzle is to evaluate your expenses. Go
back at least six months to spot spending trends. Be honest here. This exercise could
reveal trends that need to be corrected.

One way to find out where your money is going is to look at your checkbook. Then
locate your charge-card receipts and bills you've paid with cash. It may take a while to
track where your money has gone, but keep at it.

Just like assets, your expenses fall into two categories: *Fixed Expenses*—those you
must pay regularly—and *Variable Expenses*—those that come due with varying frequency or in varying amounts.

Fixed Expenses

Type of Payment	How Much/How Often	Annual Amount
INSURANCE PAYMENTS:		$
Property		$
Medical		$
Life		$
Disability		$
Dental		$
Automobile		$
TAXES:		$
Property		$
Federal		$
State		$
Social Security		$
BASIC TELEPHONE SERVICE		$
MORTGAGE OR RENT		$
		$
CAR PAYMENT(S)		$
		$
		$
OTHER LOAN PAYMENT(S)		$
		$
		$
ONGOING MEDICAL CARE		$
		$
		$
EDUCATION COSTS		$
		$
		$
BUSINESS DUES		$
		$
TITHES/PLEDGES		$
		$
		$
		$

	How Much	How Often	Annual Amount
	$		$
CHILD SUPPORT/ALIMONY	$		$
MONTHLY SAVINGS PLAN	$		$
	$		$
	$		$
OTHER FIXED EXPENSES	$		$
	$		$
	$		$
	$		$
TOTAL FIXED EXPENSES	$		$

Variable Expenses

Because these expenses vary in frequency and/or amount, it's important to know approximately how much they cost per year and to estimate how much they cost you a month. Going back through your records for six months or even a year will give you a good idea of how much these expenses are. Again, be as accurate as possible.

Type of Payment	Per Month Estimate	Annual Amount
UTILITY COSTS:	$	$
Water	$	$
Electricity	$	$
Natural Gas	$	$
Sewer	$	$
Propane	$	$
Heating Oil	$	$
Other	$	$
Long Distance Telephone Service	$	$
ROUTINE HOME MAINTENANCE	$	$
FOOD	$	$
CLOTHING	$	$
LAUNDRY/CLEANING SUPPLIES	$	$
GIFTS (BIRTHDAYS, ETC.)	$	$
TRANSPORTATION	$	$
Gasoline/Diesel Fuel	$	$
Repairs/Maintenance	$	$
Parking/Tolls	$	$

	Per Month Estimate	Annual Amount
Train/Bus/Other Public Transportation	$	$
License/Taxes	$	$
CHILDREN	$	$
Allowances	$	$
Lunches	$	$
Lessons/Sports Fees	$	$
	$	$
PERSONAL CARE	$	$
VACATIONS	$	$
ENTERTAINMENT	$	$
Movies/Cultural Events	$	$
Sporting Events	$	$
Hobbies	$	$
Eating Out	$	$
Books/Music	$	$
Club Memberships	$	$
Baby-sitters	$	$
	$	$
	$	$
UNREIMBURSED MEDICAL:	$	$
Dental Care	$	$
Eye Care	$	$
Prescriptions	$	$
Office Visits	$	$
Lab/X-ray	$	$
	$	$
	$	$
	$	$
CHARITABLE GIFTS	$	$
	$	$
	$	$
	$	$
	$	$
MISCELLANEOUS	$	$
	$	$
	$	$

	$	$
	$	$
	$	$
TOTAL VARIABLE EXPENSES	$	$

Now calculate your total expenses by adding your:

Total Fixed Expenses to your $_____

Total Variable Expenses $_____

This gives you your Total Expenses $_____

DETERMINE YOUR ANNUAL INCOME

Now it's time to record and compute your annual income:

Income Source	How Much/How Often	Annual Amount
GROSS WAGES		$
		$
		$
		$
		$
TIPS		$
ROYALTIES		$
SAVINGS/INVESTMENTS:		$
Interest		$
Interest		$
Dividends		$
Dividends		$
Annuity Payments		$
		$
		$
PENSION		$
CHILD SUPPORT/ALIMONY		$
SOCIAL SECURITY PAYMENTS		$
TRUST FUNDS		$
RENT PAID TO YOU		$
OTHER SOURCES:		$
		$

		$
		$
TOTAL INCOME		$_____

MAKE YOUR SPENDING PLAN WORK FOR YOU

Here's the test: How well do your expenses and income match up?

List your Annual Income $_____
Subtract your Annual Expenses $_____
What is the difference between your Income and Expenses? $_____

If you are spending more than you earn, don't panic! And if you are earning more than you spend, don't go on a spending spree! Whatever situation you find yourself in, you now have the information you need to develop a workable spending plan that will help you achieve your financial goals. The key now is to use the information wisely.

If you spend more than you earn, you *must* make adjustments in your expenses or your income so that you can at least break even and make forward progress in paying off your liabilities. For help in this area, we suggest that you consult one of the many resources on designing a spending plan,[1] work with a financial counselor (perhaps one in your church), or seek the help of a trustworthy and financially wise friend.

If you have more income than expenses, you also would be wise to review your expenses to see which can be decreased. A spending plan will help you adjust to your new goals and show where to allocate your resources. Because you have excess resources, you have very important choices to make. Will you use those resources to:

✓ Eliminate your liabilities?
✓ Add to your assets?
✓ Increase your giving?

Tips for Setting Up and Maintaining a Spending Plan

Once you have developed a workable spending plan, stick to it! The following tips will help:

✱ Spend time each week monitoring your income and expenses. If you are spending more than you expected in one area, where can you cut back in another area? Remember: the spending plan is a flexible tool; it's not cast in concrete.

* Consider the "big picture." The spending plan isn't designed to make you account for every nickel; it's designed to help you gain control of your financial situation.

* If you are married, evaluate the spending plan with your spouse. It's important that both of you agree on its value.

* Ensure that your spending plan reflects the needs of individual family members. One child may need more money for sports equipment, for example.

* Be conservative in estimating income. If more money comes in than you expect, great. But if it doesn't, you'll be in stronger financial shape.

* Give each family member a little money (an allowance) to spend that doesn't have to be accounted for.

* Set aside money for taxes when your income first comes in, and don't use it for anything else.

* Revise the spending plan as your needs/goals/wants change.

* As you cut spending, remove money from a number of categories instead of dramatically reducing one category (unless it's superfluous).

* Stick with your spending plan until your income and expenses are well under control and you can follow the plan naturally. If at any time you begin to lose control of your spending, return to the basics again.

Anticipate Changes in Projected Income and Expenses

Remember, your spending plan is a tool to help you gain and maintain control of your financial situation. At times your financial situation may change, perhaps due to circumstances beyond your control. Done properly, a spending plan will help you anticipate and prepare for those changes.

How might your income change during the coming months or years? (Salary freeze? Possible layoff? Anticipated retirement? Plan to earn extra income?) Describe what you see happening—good and bad—and how much money you think will be involved:

_____ $_____

_____ $_____

_____ $_____

_____ $_____

_____ $_____

What adjustments in your spending plan will help you prepare for each of these possibilities? _____

_____

_____

List all of the special expenses that you anticipate paying within the next year. (These might include car repairs, an extended vacation, buying a car, paying for an operation or dental work, college tuition, a major home repair, and so on.) Write down how much you think each of these expenses will cost and, if possible, when it might come up:

_____ $_____

_____ $_____

_____ $_____

_____ $_____

_____ $_____

_____ $_____

TOTAL ANTICIPATED EXPENSES WITHIN ONE YEAR: $_____

Divide the sum of these anticipated expenses by twelve: _____

This is the amount of money you'll need to add to your monthly fixed expenses in order to cover these future expenses.

Note: It would also be wise to anticipate additional long-term expenses (such as auto purchases or college tuition) that may not be due within the year, but will arise in two, three, or five years. Go through the same process you completed for one-year future expenses and determine the amount of money you must set aside each month in order to cover them.

There are great rewards for doing this. Think, for example, how nice it would be if the next time you need to buy a car you have cash on hand to pay for all (or at least most) of it!

Which expenses do you pay quarterly, semiannually, or annually (such as estimated taxes, insurance premiums, and/or property taxes)?

_____ $_____

_____ $_____

_____ $_____

_____ $_____

TOTAL ESTIMATED PAYMENTS (QUARTERLY, SEMIANNUAL, ETC.) $_____

Divide the sum of these estimated payments by twelve: _____
Add this amount of money to your monthly fixed expenses so you won't be caught short when these payments come due.

List at least three advantages of being able to pay for anticipated expenses and payments as well as unexpected emergencies out of your existing funds rather than having to borrow from a financial institution, family member, or friend.

1. _____

2. _____

3. _____

---

1. See Ron Blue, *Master Your Money* (Nashville: Nelson, 1986); and Larry Burkett, *A Family Budgeting Guide* (Chicago: Moody, 1990).

13
Building Relational Riches: Free or Low-Cost Family Activities

Our culture is entertainment-oriented. We can choose from thousands of video movies at a corner rental store. Malls offer an array of activities and buying options. Theater complexes typically present us with four, six, or even ten movie options. And on it goes. . . . Faced with so many entertainment choices, we easily can focus on what we can *do* instead of who we can *be* with others. Critics of culture point out that many of us have, indeed, lost our ability to relate to one another, especially family members, in intimate ways.

Life doesn't have to be this way. Two friends of ours, Doug and Jan, decided to reverse the typical relational trends in their family life. "We wanted to spend more time together, to learn how to have fun together as a family," Doug told us. "We realized that we needed to practice and learn that. It's easy for families to use activities as a substitute for deep relationships, and we were doing that, too. So we stopped long enough to ask ourselves what we felt quality of life should consist of . . . and began to focus on relationships with one another."

What's important isn't just that families do things together, it's that they enjoy participating in life with one another. Not long ago, our daughter said, "Mom, let's work on the puzzle together and talk." That's where relational riches blossom—not just in the activities we do, but in what we share through those activities. That's when the activities we enjoy become an expression of our relationship, not simply a *substitute* for relationship.

Many of these friendship and family-building activities cost little; others are free. As you read this chapter, consider how you can add free or low-cost, relationship-building activities to your life and the lives of others around you.

If you have children and/or family members in the local area, how many hours do you spend with them each week? _____

During the time you spend together, what activities do you typically do? _____

_____

_____

_____

How satisfied are you with the level of personal interaction that takes place during these times? _____

_____

_____

In what ways might that interaction be deepened? _____

_____

_____

Looking back on your own "growing up years," which activities or times with your parent(s) or extended family members meant the most to you? _____

_____

_____

What made those times so special? Was it the activities? Was it their participation in something you enjoyed? Be specific. _____

_____

_____

THE CHALLENGE OF BUILDING RELATIONSHIPS

It's not easy to make free and low-cost family activities fun and challenging and to develop strong relationships with our children, friends, and with God. It takes purpose, planning, and determination.

In what ways has your family used activities as a substitute for relationship?

_____

Which daily/weekly events in your life create a hectic pace that negatively affects your ability to build relationships with family and/or friends? _____

_____

_____

Describe what you think "rich" relationships with your family members would look like. _____

_____

_____

Write down three steps you will take this week in order to schedule more time for building "relational riches" among your family and/or close friends:

1. _____

2. _____

3. _____

If family members live in your area, and it's appropriate, ask them what type of relationship-building activities they'd enjoy doing with you. Record their answers below. If possible, build these activities into your schedule in the near future.

Note: Watching a movie doesn't count, but having lunch together after a movie would. Remember, the emphasis is on relationship-building activities, not just on activities.

Name	Relationship builder	When to do it

IDEAS FOR RELATIONSHIP-BUILDING ACTIVITIES

Sometimes the simplest activities can be the most fun: a walk in a forest, for example, or a trip to the zoo. Following are some ideas on which you and your family/friends can build. Be creative! Have fun thinking about activities that draw on the personal interests of family members and the strengths of your particular area of the country. If you live in a cold-weather climate, you might include sledding or ice skating. If you live near the ocean, you might go beachcombing or hunt for sand dollars. If you live in a major urban center, you might enjoy ethnic or multicultural festivals. At the end of each section, add your own ideas.

Games

Games fill an important role in developing physical and intellectual skills, stimulating creative ability, and deepening our relational experience. Challenging games develop thinking ability. Easy games provide a setting for quiet conversation. Silly games provide a healthy dose of laughter. Team games develop cooperation. Physical games develop strength and coordination. As you think of games your family and/or friends can enjoy together, also consider ways to make the most of the relational opportunities each type of activity provides.

✗ Play yard games such as croquet, lawn darts, tag.

✗ Enjoy field or park games such as baseball, football, soccer, or Frisbee.

✗ Have a water-balloon fight or squirt-gun battle.

✗ Put puzzles together. (We purchased a box of about thirty puzzles at an auction—for a dollar!)

✗ Pull out your favorite board game, or make your own!

✗ Take on the challenge of becoming highly skilled at a complex game such as chess. This is something a parent and child can enjoy learning together.

✗ Participate in the imitations of real life that children enjoy. These include "store," "hospital," "restaurant," "fireman," and "school," just to name a few. Help young children make and find props that make these games more realistic and fun. Listen to what is said during these games—they often reveal what your child is learning about life.

✗ Select favorite stories to act out in your own theater. These can be Bible stories, fairy tales, classic adventures, or stories your family makes up. Present them in a homemade puppet theater with homemade puppets, or dress up and act out the parts yourself. These can be as simple or as complex as your family wants to make them.

✗ List three other activities that you could (or have) done with your family:

✗ _____

✗ _____

✗ _____

Crafts and Hobbies to Enjoy Together

The joy of creating something with another person is undeniable. The gift of teaching a child or helping a young person learn and perfect a new skill is a great relational gift.

- Build a birdhouse or bird feeder.
- Learn to make bread or candy together.
- If you live in a snowy region, make snow sculptures.
- Make your own cards and send them to friends.
- Draw pictures or do other art projects together.
- Make a wind chime.
- Make your own kites and fly them.
- Make Christmas or birthday gifts for friends and extended family.
- Build a go-cart, fix a bicycle, or build a tree fort.
- Explore the world around you by learning about birds, rocks, trees, edible plants, and so on. Try some scientific experiments, too!
- Make your own gift wrappings out of maps, aluminum foil, newspaper, magazine pages, and so on.
- Start learning about and collecting items of interest. Make it a game to find low-cost ways to add to your collection.
- List two crafts, hobbies, or projects you could do with family members.
- _____
- _____

Physical Activities

Many fun, physical activities encourage deeper relationships. Here are a few suggestions. Add your favorites to the list:

Activity:	Where:	Cost:
Roller-skating		$
Ice skating (indoors or out)		$
Taking a family bike hike		$
Renting a canoe or boat for a day		$
Hiking		$
Overnight camping		$
Visiting nearby playgrounds		$

Activity:	Where:	Cost:
Playing tennis, volleyball, or		$
basketball on a public court		$
Sledding or skiing		$
Competing in races together		$
Swimming		$
		$
		$
		$
		$

Great Places and Unique Opportunities

When you take the time to look for them, chances are you will find a surprising variety of free or low-cost activities to enjoy together. Check out the options available to you.

✓ List the state or national parks, historic sites, recreation areas, wildlife refuges, and/or monuments you would like to visit in your area:

_____

_____

_____

_____

_____

_____

Be sure to find out the following:

✓ If there is normally an admission charge, are there days when admission is reduced or free?
✓ What special programs, presentations, or guided tours are offered at these locations? When are they offered? What are the costs?
✓ What hours are these normally open? In season? Out of season?
✓ Are there picnic tables, fire pits, or nature trails? Is overnight camping allowed?
✓ What cultural/educational opportunities does your city offer? These may include art museums, botanical gardens, zoos, natural history museums, local history/culture museums, and/or science museums.

Place:	Location:	Hours:	Admission:

✓ Check your local calendar of events and note the parades, public exhibitions, festivals, and outdoor concerts planned for your area. Many of these are scheduled on holiday weekends and will be free. If it's an annual event, it might become a great family tradition. (Two of our favorites in Colorado are the Great Pikes Peak Cowboy Poetry Gathering and getting up at the crack of dawn for the hot-air balloon festival. They're both free!)

Event:	Date(s):	Location:	Cost:

✓ Contact your state tourism office and travel agencies to learn about free or low-cost places to visit. List the ones your family would enjoy below:

Place to visit:	Costs:	Do in a few hours?	Do in a day?	Do overnight?

✓ If you're interested in professional sports, find out about special promotions and free or reduced admission days. _____

✓ Does your state or county have an annual fair? If so, when will it be held?

_____

✓ Where is the closest working farm you could visit (assuming you don't already live on one)? _____

✓ Where is the closest park, nature trail, or river where you could walk?

_____

✓ Would your family enjoy an auction, a morning of garage sale hunting, or an afternoon at a flea market? If so, when and where?_____

✓ Where can you pick your own fruit or vegetables? _____

_____

As you can see, the opportunities for low-cost family outings are more abundant than you might at first imagine. Start planning some memorable family times today.

MAKING VACATIONS SPECIAL—AND SAVING IN THE PROCESS

Vacations are important times for families to forget about daily concerns, experience a refreshing change of pace, and focus on enjoying one another. Even if your financial resources are limited, a bit of vacation time will pay dividends in relational riches.

Which vacation has been "the best ever" for you and/or your family? _____

_____

What made that time special? _____

_____

What was the short- and long-term impact of that vacation? _____

_____

_____

Find out what each family member would most enjoy doing during your next vacation. _____

_____

How might those desires be combined into a vacation that meets the needs of the whole family? _____

_____

_____

You don't have to have a family to enjoy a vacation rich in relationships. Many people share their vacations with one or more good friends.

If you were to vacation with a friend, who would you choose? _____

_____

Where would you like to go? What would you like to do? _____

_____

_____

There are many "vacation" options from which to choose. Check the options below that appeal to you:

- ❑ Would you enjoy remaining at home but receiving no phone calls? Or seeing the local sights without feeling pressured? Try taking a vacation at home—and let people think you're gone.
- ❑ Do you have friends who live in a completely different setting (such as city condo vs. country home) with whom you could swap houses for a weekend?
- ❑ If an extended vacation is not possible, would a series of long weekends provide the relaxation and fun you need?
- ❑ If overnight hotel accommodations are too expensive, could you save money by camping? By renting a travel trailer or motor home? By renting a small cottage for a week?
- ❑ Would you enjoy a vacation that was interspersed with visits to extended family?
- ❑ Can you coordinate your vacation time with your business travel requirements?
- ❑ Would a short-term missions project meet your need for a refreshing (but demanding) change of pace?
- ❑ Other _____
- ❑ Other _____
- ❑ Other _____

Whatever options you choose, put your money-saving strategies to work. Find out about travel and accommodation discounts, off-peak savings, and make the most of your time.

OTHER WAYS TO BUILD RELATIONAL RICHES

Building relational riches isn't limited to entertaining activities with your immediate family and friends. Consider what you can to do build relationships with those in your extended family or others outside your normal circle of friends.

✓ Perform volunteer activities together as a family. Which would your family enjoy: A fund-raising walk? Planting trees? Church workdays? Special Olympics?

_____

_____

✓ Send a letter (or video) on tape to the following people: _____

_____

✓ Write a family newsletter at Christmastime or some other time of the year. Each family member can write an article, draw a picture, take photographs, and so on.

✓ Bake a special food/dessert and deliver it to the following person(s) in your neighborhood or church: _____

_____

✓ Think about which person(s) you would enjoy getting to know better during a meal and invite that person to join you. _____

✓ Invite someone you know who lives alone to join you and your family for a meal at home or at a restaurant.

✓ Invite a person from another country to join you for dinner.

✓ If you would like to learn a new skill, who might also enjoy learning that skill with you? _____

Perhaps you could take a class at your local community college, park and recreation department, or YMCA.

These are just a few ways to build relational riches within your family and community. Work at it, and you will see that relational riches are well worth your investment.

14
Why Save Money?

We began this workbook with a short chapter that discussed building a solid foundation for financial decisions. We conclude by returning to that foundation to ask a fundamental question. Why save money?

It may seem strange to ask this question at the end of this workbook. After all, saving money is good, right? We think so. Probably you do, too, or you wouldn't be using this workbook. The challenge of living smart and spending less, however, involves more than just saving money. You see, it's important for each of us to determine the priorities of our hearts, to examine our underlying reasons for saving money. As in many aspects of life, it's possible to spend less for the right reasons . . . and also for the wrong reasons.

With the exception of God, who knows everything you think and feel, you—on your own or with the help of other people—are the only one who can examine your attitudes, beliefs, and priorities related to money.

In this final section, you'll explore your real reasons for wanting to live smart and spend less. Be honest here. If you are married, answer the following questions separately and then discuss them with your spouse. You may be surprised by what you discover. If you need more room for your answers, write them on a separate sheet of paper.

Why do you want to live smart and spend less? What specific benefits or goals do you want to obtain or reach?

1. _____

2. _____

3. _____

4. _____

5. _____

6. _____

7.' _____

8. _____

9. _____

In the margin, write a "1" next to the benefit or goal that is most important to you. Then number the remaining benefits and goals in order of their importance.

What does the order of priority you assigned to your reasons for living smart and spending less reveal about you? _____

_____

_____

In what ways is your lifestyle compatible with or dissimilar to the priorities you have listed? Be honest! _____

_____

_____

In what ways is your spending (as revealed by your checkbook or charge statements) compatible with or dissimilar to the priorities you have listed? _____

_____

_____

What steps can you take to bring your life's actions more in line with your goals? (If you are married, first answer this question individually, then as a couple.) _____

_____

_____

We all hope to gain certain benefits when we save money, but we also need to consider the underlying reasons that we want or choose to save money. You may be sensing that a philosophical or spiritual statement is coming. It is, but relax. It's a simple one: *Money is a resource, and the reasons you save and spend money reveal your real life priorities and spiritual perspectives.*

Do you agree with this statement? Why or why not? _____

_____

Every dollar you save through living smart is a resource. When you access greater resources, you can make more choices regarding what you'll do with your dollars and cents. That's why it is important for you to discover the real reasons you choose to save money. What your smart living truly accomplishes is determined by the priorities of your heart. How much you save is actually less important than how you use the new resources available to you because of your choices.

A MOMENT OF REFLECTION

On page 255 of our book *Living Smart, Spending Less* we list more than two dozen reasons why people save. We have reproduced that checklist below[1] for you to read. Please put a check mark inside each box that applies to you. Again, be honest.

- ❑ I want to be like other people I know.
- ❑ I want more security.
- ❑ I want to feel good about myself.
- ❑ I want others to feel good about me.
- ❑ I want to be able to help others.
- ❑ I'm afraid that unless I maintain a certain lifestyle, people won't think I'm successful.
- ❑ I tend to gauge how well I'm doing in life by what I own or what I've purchased.
- ❑ I don't want to be hassled by creditors.
- ❑ I feel guilty about how I've spent my money in the past and want to turn things around.
- ❑ I want to be in control of my life, and having money will help me to do that.
- ❑ I want to provide a better living for my family.
- ❑ I want the freedom that money can bring.
- ❑ I'm tired of watching my dollars disappear with little to show for my efforts.
- ❑ I want the way I live to count for something beyond myself.
- ❑ I'm not sure why I want to save money; it just sounds like a good thing to do.
- ❑ I want to be in financial control of my life, to be independently wealthy.
- ❑ Maybe money doesn't buy happiness, but I'd like to have enough money to find that out for myself.
- ❑ I want to honor God by the way I live.
- ❑ I'm afraid of what life can dish out, and having money will help insulate me from what could happen.
- ❑ I enjoy reaching my goals, and having money is one of my key goals.
- ❑ I earn money by using my skills, so why not use skills in saving it?

❑ If I save a dollar here, I can spend a dollar there.

❑ I don't like what I see happening in the government, and if everything collapses I don't want to go down the tubes too.

❑ I want options in life so I can explore and use my gifts and abilities more fully.

❑ I want to prove something to my family.

❑ I really don't care about saving money (I'd rather spend it), but my spouse (or parent) is pressuring me to save.

❑ I believe that what I have is a gift to be used wisely.

❑ I want more money because it will open doors for me.

❑ If I can't make a lot of money, maybe I can move up the ladder a rung.

❑ _____. (Fill in your own reason.)

Which of your priorities and attitudes are reflected in this list? _____

_____

_____

_____

Are you comfortable or uncomfortable with them? Why? _____

_____

Were you surprised by any of your feelings? If so, which ones? _____

_____

_____

THE LAWS THAT THROW A WRENCH INTO OUR PLANS

No matter how well each of us succeeds at making wise financial choices—at living smart and spending less—we must recognize and make choices based on the following five laws. These laws remain constant no matter what we do or how many material possessions we own.

Law One: We all will die one day.

Death is inescapable. No matter how much we've saved, how often we exercise, and how careful we are, we all will die someday. No matter how much we accumulate, we can't take it with us.

In what ways do your financial choices have eternal consequences? _____

_____

_____

Law Two: We cannot control life's circumstances.

The amount of money we accumulate can't protect us from difficult circumstances that inevitably arise.

Do you believe in the truth of this law? Why or why not? _____
_____
_____

To what extent does fear influence your view of finances and saving money? _____
_____
_____

Law Three: Money itself cannot provide lasting inner peace and joy.

Many song lyrics have communicated that money alone is not enough to win someone's heart, much less lead to a deeper sense of meaning and purpose. Likewise, the business world is strewn with tired people who believed that they'd be able to fill a void deep inside if they earned so much a year and gained the trappings of wealth. Personally, we've discovered that only a relationship with God through Christ can provide lasting peace and joy.

In your opinion, what can money provide? _____
_____
_____

What, for you, gives lasting peace and joy? _____
_____
_____

Law Four: Enough is seldom enough.

Like an addiction to alcohol or drugs, having money often fuels the desire to acquire even more money. And that desire to acquire more typically leads to additional financial pressures.

In what ways has obtaining money been consuming for you? _____
_____
_____
_____

Just as spending money carelessly can ruin lives and families, being miserly can lead to misfortune and selfishness. And greed, which can be easily hidden in a culture that tends to worship "success" and individual achievement, leads to great pain.

Do you agree or disagree with the two sentences above? Why or why not? _____

_____

_____

Law Five: Money can be used to create good or bad consequences.

Money itself is a "neutral" resource. What we do with money can result in good or bad consequences. Remember, the apostle Paul said that the *love* of money is a root of all evil, not money itself (1 Timothy 6:10).

In what ways have you seen money used to create good consequences? _____

_____

_____

To create bad consequences? _____

_____

_____

How might you use your money to create good consequences in your family and/or community? _____

_____

_____

A FINAL QUESTION

As you save money, you will have to choose how to use the money you save. Will you help a family pay for necessary medical care? Help to stock a local food bank? Help a financially strapped college student with tuition? _____

List specific ways in which you plan to use the money you save as you apply the principles and tips in this workbook: _____

_____

_____

_____

_____

_____

You have successfully worked through this workbook. In light of what you've learned, consider how the following story may pertain to you.

While waiting in line at the airport in Madras, India, about ten years ago, Stephen noticed several people going to the front of the line to board the aircraft. One of them was Mother Teresa, the nun who received the Nobel Peace Prize in 1979 for her work in the slums of Calcutta, India.

She sat across the aisle from him, looking as frail as her photographs in the magazines. Stephen couldn't help but glance at her from time to time.

As the jet reached cruising altitude, a flight attendant served juice and rolls. Stephen eagerly bolted them down, then heard a rustling noise. Mother Teresa was carefully wrapping up the rolls.

She noticed his gaze, gave him a warm smile, and said, "For the children. For the children."

How are you using the resources God has given you? To whom are you offering the bread we have to share? Perhaps, just as Jesus multiplied a few fish and pieces of bread in order to feed many people,[2] He will use some of the money you save in special ways—even if you start with only two small rolls.

It's your choice.

1. Stephen and Amanda Sorenson, *Living Smart, Spending Less* (Chicago: Moody, 1993). Used by permission.
2. Matthew 14:13–21.